IT'S NOT JUST GYMNASTICS; IT'S LIFE

The Experiences and Insights of Olympic Gymnast Lance Ringnald

Written by:
LANCE RINGNALD
with Stacey Lake

ISBN: 146815124X
ISBN13: 9781468151244

Dedicated,
with loving gratitude,
to our parents, brothers,
and amazing friends.

CONTENTS

A Note from Lance .... *vii*

1. Early Childhood 1
2. Starting Gymnastics 7
3. Growing Up in the Sport 11
4. Major Competitions Begin 20
5. Changes and Trials 29
6. 1988 Olympics in Seoul, Korea 44
7. After the Olympics 55
8. Goodwill Games 63
9. Overcoming Injury 71
10. Getting Through the Trials 80
11. Deep Thoughts, and the '92 Olympics 90
12. Last Days of Competition 98

Photo Gallery *105*

13. Life After Competition 111
14. The Need for New Challenges 119
15. Developing the "Lance Ringnald Show" ... 129
16. Frequently Asked Questions 136
17. Opinions and Insights 152
18. Concluding Thoughts 176

Afterthoughts: Personal Mottos and Truths *179*

A Note from Lance

Though my book has an official dedication, I am keenly aware that there are many people I need to acknowledge by name when it comes to the story I am privileged to tell. When considering all those who have influenced me, and when trying to choose which ones to mention, I cannot help but think about how those I choose will feel when they read this. Flattered, maybe? Happy? Proud? No matter what emotion is evoked in them, I believe it may not equal the appreciation and gratitude I have for them. The process is tricky. There are many people and experiences that contribute to one man's accomplishments and character. There could even be a random person who casually speaks a word or idea to someone, but it may be a significant piece—even the last piece—of a one thousand-word puzzle. It may trigger a thought that changes the way one sees the world. Seemingly small actions can change the entire course of a person's life. In so doing, they can cause that person to change the lives of others. It's a giant ripple effect. So, how do we choose those to whom we show our gratitude in a book? Hopefully, we do it as we do most things in life—the best that we can.

With that said, I wish to offer my additional words of appreciation to:

My family, first and foremost. Without them, I would not have this story to tell. I have been very fortunate to have an exceptionally reasonable, loving, caring, and simply fun family. I am an equal mix of my mother and father, and I am happy for the characteristics of each of them that have stuck with me. Thank you, Mom, Dad, and Joe.

My coaches. Ed Burch coached me through both Olympics and three World Championship teams. He was crazy enough to believe anything was possible, and he has the gift of bringing out the full potential in his athletes. Bill Foster offered a lot of wisdom and encouragement, and he helped construct my routines to earn the highest possible scores. Rick Summerhayes, Wayne Dixon, Doug Fitzgerald, and Lance King all coached me at one time or another, and they all added a great deal to my gymnastics development. Finally, I must not forget all the other coaches with whom I crossed paths over the years who graciously shared their expertise to help me improve. Thank you—each one of you made a difference.

My biggest rivals and closest teammates, Trent Dimas and Chainey Umphrey. We were much better gymnasts because of our influence on each other.

My fellow competitors in gymnastics. They were my competition, my teammates, and my friends.

My co-author and dear friend, Stacey Lake. Without her, this book would have never been finished!

Those who are no longer with us. I have known many, and my life has been touched by many, whose lives have been cut short. From our perspective, their lives ended far too soon. But, they still caused many ripples in the lives of others. We would have liked more time with them; they will not be forgotten.

IT'S NOT JUST GYMNASTICS; IT'S LIFE

Chapter 1

EARLY CHILDHOOD

I f you find yourself sitting down to read this book, it probably means you have some interest in gymnastics, in the Olympics, or in the deep, psychological inner workings of a person who has dedicated his life to the pursuit of. . .ok, we won't go that far. You are reading for whatever reason, perhaps simply for entertainment, so allow me to introduce myself and attempt to entertain you. My name is Lance Ringnald, a.k.a. gymnast, Olympian, juggler, pianist, singer, silk-worker, entertainer, and now, writer. When it comes right down to it, it is because of my time as an entertainer on cruise ships that this book has come into being. I meet many people, and many people have asked questions about my life and my experiences in gymnastics, especially in the Olympics. Realizing the interest was there, I eventually felt compelled to answer all those questions in written form. So, it begins. . .

I was born on June 13, 1970, in Des Moines, Iowa. My parents are Paul and Roxann Ringnald. I was the second child, born in the shadow of my older brother, Joe, two and one-half years my senior. I was brought up in a good family setting, and it was my parents who taught me many of the values and principles I still practice now. Because both of my parents were gymnasts in college (that's how they met), it is almost as if I had kind of a genetic resource to the world of gymnastics—one that kicked in even before I was born. I guess I didn't have a choice, and I can't tell you how glad I am about that.

I can't exactly say I grew up as a "normal" kid, because who is to say what "normal" really means? I do know that as a young kid, around eight or so, I was very hyperactive. I would literally break the springs in the couches and furniture around the house just bouncing around. I had a very potent imagination, even among my peers, and I seemed to daydream, living in my own world a lot. I loved kung fu movies and any type of superhero movies. I wanted to be like the characters I saw in those films. Once, when my mom asked me what I wanted to be when I grew up, I responded, "I want to be Inframan!" <u>Inframan</u> was what could be considered a cheesy Japanese superhero movie, where a brilliant scientist turned an average man into a super-powerful-robot-man to save the world. (Kind of a Japanese six million dollar man meets Jet Li kind of thing. Just the thing for a young kid to idolize!) Inframan could fly and flip around and had super-strength, so of course I wanted to be just like him. What "normal" kid would not want to be like that?

Anyway, when I ran around the house and bounced off the furniture, Inframan was who I imagined myself to be. Having a very visual imagination made me creative, which is an asset in many ways. It led to lots of activity, lots of stories in my head, and lots of fun. But, I cannot say that it led to a successful academic career. I never was a very good student. I had trouble paying attention long enough to grasp any subject that did not appeal to me. Throughout my schooling, in fact, my rhythm was as follows: if I liked a subject or class and was interested, I would get an "A". If I did not like the subject or class, I would just somehow manage to complete the minimum to pass. My parents actually had me psychologically tested throughout my schooling, looking for learning disabilities out of concern for my lack of attention, for my sporadic lack of comprehension, and for writing upside down and backwards. They probably longed for a positive diagnosis so there would be something to blame—some justification for my "issues." But instead, the findings were that I had no discernable learning disabilities. Even so, a consensus was reached that I did, indeed, have an unusual way of learning. My parents were told that a teacher may try fifty different ways to teach me one thing, and I just might not get it. That was absolutely true. But, more often than not, maybe a week or a month following some area of instruction, a light bulb would suddenly go on in my head and I would gain a full understanding. I don't know how or why, but the knowledge would suddenly be there, and once it arrived, it would never leave. This meant that I had to learn things in a specific way or I would have trouble understanding. It was just not clear what that specific way actually was.

Over time, it became apparent that I learned best by visual perception. That worked very well for me most of the time. One exception to this came at an early age, before I could read. I was with my grandmother at a restaurant, and I had to go to the restroom. The restrooms were only a short distance from our table, so my grandmother decided it was fine for me to go alone. I asked how I would know which door was the men's room. Nana told me that one of the doors would have a long word on it (women) and the other door would have a short word on it (men). I was good with that and went confidently to the end of the hallway where the doors were. Shortly after that, however, I returned to the table very confused. I told Nana that I couldn't go to the bathroom because there were three doors, not two, and I didn't know which one to go into. I explained that two of the doors had short words, and one had a longer word. Nana got up and went with me. She started laughing when she saw the problem. One door said "Women", one said "Men", and the third door said "Exit". Nana was really glad I hadn't chosen that one. Anyway, it became clear that if I could picture what I was being told in my mind, I could understand it very well. On the other hand, if obstacles—or unforeseen, nasty tricks—came my way, I might have a bit of trouble.

Visual learner that I was, gymnastics fit my learning style perfectly. But, even in the gym, there were obstacles. One painful, embarrassing learning incident happened one night at gymnastics class when I was ten years old. My coach asked me to go over to the clock and see what time it was. When I got to the clock he called over to me and asked the time. I told him, "The long hand is on the three and the short hand is a little after the seven." I gave him the information, but it did not register as a "time" in my mind. I should have known how to tell time by that age, but facts are facts—I didn't. My brain was very selective about what it wanted to learn. Again, if I enjoyed learning something, I would learn it very well and without difficulty. But, if there was something I didn't find crucial, I had a hard time forcing my brain to take it in. Telling time fell under the "I don't care" category. Who really cares what time it is? Of course, after the embarrassing moment at the gym, I began to care a little bit more. Thus, learning to tell time became a higher priority and I learned to tell time very quickly after that. However, I dragged my feet on mastering the months of the year for a very long time.

So, with that little bit of insight into my unusual mind, let us return to a question that commonly comes my way. Apart from my parents' DNA, how did I become involved in gymnastics? To be honest, I was introduced to gymnastics accidentally when I was eight years old. I was living in Omaha, Nebraska, and I had just completed my first day of third grade. After school, I was riding my bike around the neighborhood. I was a cool kid, by the way—cool enough to have a mini-goose BMX—an "off-road" bike. Being eight and very excited to have finished my first day of school, I had a lot of energy to wear off. And, to make this particular scene just a little more dramatic, just down the street from my house was a street where a girl I liked lived. Somehow, I found myself riding by her house a lot. That day, I was riding really fast—"Inframan" fast—on my cool BMX bike when I left her street and rode onto the main street. I was always good at looking to the right, but sometimes I did not do so well at looking to the left. That is one drawback of being young, I suppose. One tends to forget those minor details. I did look back to the left just in time to notice a car coming very quickly toward me. Time started moving very slowly. My brain almost seemed to stop. It was inevitable that I was going to hit this car or be hit. I remember feeling totally helpless. Knowing that this accident was going to happen, I gripped the handlebars as hard as I could. Everything was moving extremely slowly. My front tire hit right in front of the car's front tire, and I was launched off my bike and over the hood of the car. I was told later that my body tumbled one and a half times, with arms and legs going everywhere. Everyone knows that what goes up must come down, so after my one and a half, I met the pavement with my chin first, followed quickly by the side of my head. The result was that I fractured my chin and jaw, and six of my baby teeth exploded out of my mouth—along with several fillings. This all seemed to happen in an instant. However, I continued to skid and roll in the street and was left with lacerations and bruising on my back, side, and stomach. I never lost consciousness, and I remember crying for my mom and trying to get up to run home. I could see several teeth that looked like little white marbles, and blood was pouring from my chin onto the pavement. A friend of mine tried to hold me down and keep me calm. My bike was mangled and missing the front tire. It was beyond repair. Another friend who saw the accident ran to my house to get my parents. When he told them what had happened, my mom hit the ground running—something she told me later—praying that her legs wouldn't give out from under her. She just needed to get to me as fast as she could.

My mom arrived, and when she saw all the people standing around, it terrified her. Then she saw me and heard me crying and knew I was conscious, which helped to calm her. And, knowing she was there helped to calm me. She checked me for broken bones and asked where I hurt. Then she stopped the bleeding from my chin with towels brought to her by a neighbor. Just as she asked if an ambulance had been called, we could all hear the sirens. The paramedics arrived and moved quickly. They checked me out and stabilized my neck, and then they loaded me into the ambulance. Mom rode with me. Dad had to follow in his car because he had to find someone to care for my brother, Joe, before he could leave. Joe refused to ride in the ambulance or go to the hospital because he was afraid I would die. I guess his fears made sense; it was a very bad accident. And really, he's a good brother—always thinking of others!

At the hospital, the emergency room doctors and nurses took wonderful care of me. I was examined, x-rayed, and stitched up. I ended up with thirty-two stitches in my chin! I was incredibly lucky that my injuries weren't worse. After getting situated in my hospital room, there was great relief that I would be all right. Because of my age and the way my jaw had been broken, I didn't have to have it wired, and the doctors said that my jaw and my chin should heal just fine. I spent one night in the hospital and was out of school for the next two weeks before healing enough to return to normal third grade life. My perception of the entire event was mixed up. In the hospital I had told my parents that I was never going to ride a bike again and that I would never again go trick-or-treating. At the time, there was a lot of talk about candy being tainted or needles being found in Halloween treats. I think that at that point, for the first time in my young life, I felt vulnerable and not as invincible as I once had, so my logic was to avoid anything that could possibly (though very unlikely) bring me pain or place me in danger. My "logic" might have made me a bit more cautious, but of course, I went on to do both activities again. Also, because of the accident, my new life was launched; I had done my first front flip!

Chapter 2

STARTING GYMNASTICS

Though my flip over the car was a spectacular initiation into the world of gymnastics, my true involvement in the sport did not begin until a few years later, when I was ten years old. We had moved to Iowa when I was nine, and my dad would often entertain me by teaching me basic gymnastics tricks—in our family room. I quickly learned to love that feeling of flipping around and trying, as always, to become a superhero. We would take the cushions off the couches and lay them on the floor, and Dad would flip me onto them. The more he did this, the more aware I became of what my body was actually doing in the air. Though it was all fun and games, I now see the value of every toss. I give that point of my life a lot of credit for the early development of my air sense, something that would later grow to be above average, even when compared to that of my Olympic peers.

In our playtime, Dad helped me to flip over and over, and he eventually taught me how to do a back handspring. That is when people jump backwards to their hands in a handstand position, and then spring up to their feet again. I was only nine years old, and I can still remember how excited I was to be able to do this trick. When I got older and became a more accomplished gymnast, I often looked back at old video of the back handspring Dad taught me and laughed at how bad my technique was and how poorly I flipped over (as if anyone did any skill perfectly or even moderately well the first time attempted). It really did not matter, though. I felt like Inframan, and my imagination just took off. My pride took over as well; I remember firmly believing that I was the ONLY nine year old in the world who could do a trick like that. I realize now that there are four and five year olds who can do it, but in my nine-year-old mind, I had become a superhero!

With my new skill learned, I was hooked. My school was very close to home, and after school I would stay a little later and play on the playground and on the grass practicing back handsprings and other tricks Dad had helped me to learn in the family room. I knew then that I wanted to learn more and more and that I loved gymnastics. I loved the sport back then, before I even started taking gymnastics classes, for the same reasons I still love it today – for that sensation of flying and having complete (usually) control over my body. I also love it for the challenge of always having something else to learn or to improve upon, and of rarely reaching perfection but always striving for it. Yes, those first back handsprings were sloppy, but my enthusiasm and my love for training and learning would, over time, help a great deal in correcting any bad habits I formed as a nine-year-old superhero.

When I was ten years old, Mom and Dad decided to sign me up for gymnastics classes after seeing an ad on TV for *Stars Gymnastics Academy*. I began my training by attending gymnastics classes every Tuesday and Thursday for two hours. I was part of a group that included four other boys. The entire gymnastics program at *Stars* actually revolved around girls' gymnastics, and I think that out of about two hundred students in the program, there were no more than ten boys. Of the six events in men's gymnastics (floor, pommel horse, rings, vault, parallel bars and high bar), they did not have the high bar—the event on which I would one day become world champion—or the rings. It did not matter at my age and level; I was there to flip around and to continue my training as a superhero. Learning was the side effect.

I became so obsessed with gymnastics that I would do my stretches in the back of the car as my mom drove me to class. Once we arrived, I would run far ahead of Mom into the gym, where I could not have been happier. For those two hours, I was Inframan in training. Every new trick I learned was one I deemed the best trick in the world, and I felt very special to be able to learn what I considered to be such great tricks.

My passion, or obsession, carried over to every part of my life. On the projector, I would watch Mom's and Dad's old gymnastics films of famous gymnasts. Any time there was gymnastics on TV, no matter how late it might have been, my parents would make an exception to bedtime rules and let me watch. In school, I would write down on paper the areas in my gymnastics where I could one day earn high scores if I would just point my toes on a certain part of the trick, or kick harder on a swing to go higher, or run faster to get more power.

I think Mom and Dad really liked the fact that I had such an intense love for the sport. I am sure they would have preferred that I had a little better balance between school and gymnastics, but they saw how happy I was when I was doing gymnastics, and that made them happy, too. If the idle mind is the devil's playground, I had no playground available to him. I was never idle because of gymnastics, and I think Mom and Dad liked that a lot. They saw gymnastics as something positive, where I could grow and apply my youthful energy. They were firm believers, especially Dad, in involving both my brother and me in activities that would give us focus and tap into our passions. They knew that those were the activities that would contribute to the building of our character.

My "character" construction was well under way. After I had been in gymnastics classes for a couple of months, the gym acquired rings and a high bar, so I started learning tricks on all six events. My first coach, Rick Summerhayes, had a lasting impact on me. He had been a college gymnast, and he was very enthusiastic about teaching his gymnastics students. One thing that stood out about Rick, besides his red hair, was that he had really big biceps and was very strong from his competitive days as a gymnast. Rick was the one who led me to my next stepping-stone, which, aside from learning many new gymnastics skills and making them better over time, was my first competition. Luckily, it was only a tumbling meet, and tumbling was my best event at that time. I was not that good on the other events yet, and I believe I would have done poorly.

The tumbling competition took place in Waterloo, Iowa, and it was called the Waterloo Tumbling Championships. We had to do two different routines down the mat. One routine was called the compulsory tumbling pass, and it was the same for everybody. The other routine was called the optional tumbling pass, and we could do our choice and highest level of tumbling. I had never competed before, and I was surprised at how nervous I was before performing. However, once I started my routines, I was much more comfortable and did very well with both of them. I got third in the compulsories and first in the optionals. This was the first time I had ever gotten a trophy. I had never thought about that part of competition, and I was very happy to have done the routines I practiced doing and to have won something for doing them! I had gone into that competition with child-like innocence, not knowing what to expect, and in thinking back, I realize what a powerful impact it had on me to win, and to have something to show for what I did. I knew I wanted to win more things. This was only a tumbling competition and again, as the sport of gymnastics is made up of five other events, I knew I had to learn more on the other events to truly take part in the sport.

My obsession that had begun quite by accident had been fed by quests for superheroism, and it would only increase as time went by.

Chapter 3

GROWING UP IN THE SPORT

After I had taken gymnastics classes for about a year, I was improving quickly and showing a lot of promise. So, when my dad got a job promotion and I found out we were moving to Waco, Texas, I was not thrilled. I was really happy with my gym in Iowa, and I certainly did not want to leave or change gyms. I was eleven years old, and I was settled in. But, my coach, Rick, assured me they had a lot of places where I could take gymnastics in Texas, and he guessed they would even be more modern and better equipped than where I was. He was right. Mom and Dad quickly found a new gym for me to go to in Texas, and when I started taking classes there, I could really see how underdeveloped that little gym in Iowa had been.

The new gym, *Spenco*, was like a high tech playground for me. There were two of each apparatus, and there was much more space than what I was used to. Also, there was a pit! A pit is a large hole in the floor filled with cubes of foam. Events like high bar, vault, tumbling, parallel bars, and rings were all practiced over or near the pit. Many gymnastics skills require much repetition in order for the gymnasts to get the feel of them and to understand how the body twists and flips correctly. In the beginning of learning a difficult skill, it is common to get lost in the air while flipping and twisting around, which often means landing very badly. The pit was a great tool for safety. This was my first experience with a gymnastics pit, and I loved it! Even if I landed on my head, the foam blocks were soft enough to not hurt or cause injury. This took the fear factor away from doing a skill for the first time. I could master my landings into the pit, and eventually, I would learn a skill better and a mat would be placed over the pit so it was still very soft but allowed for a sturdier landing. When I progressed at the skill, I would take it from the pit to the normal floor mat and the coach would stand by, just in case I needed an assist. Finally, I would be ready to execute the skill all on my own.

Now, for the rookies or for the obsessively curious, it is important to note that all of gymnastics is based on progression. For example, gymnasts might begin by learning a perfect backward roll. Then, they learn how to jump properly to do that backward roll in the air, which is a back flip, also called a back somersault. When they master the back flip, the next step might be to learn it in the straight body position (a back layout), then with a twist (a full), then with two twists and perhaps, eventually, with a double flip. This is how gymnastics is really developed. Through repetition of the correct techniques, the body develops a keen memory of how to perform those techniques. Then, the body gets stronger, faster, and more aware of how to best execute a skill. This is what I got to experience, because with the advantages of a great gymnastics facility and of several different coaches who were very experienced in the world of gymnastics, I progressed quickly, growing stronger, faster, and more aware of my body as it would hurl through the air.

During my first year in Texas, I took full advantage of the better equipment, I trained for around two hours a day, five days a week, and I got better and better. I had come in strong on floor exercise, and the other five events grew much stronger for me during that first year there. However, though I was learning more and more gymnastics skills, I had still had only one experience in competition. Then, at the age of twelve, I had my first gymnastics competition in which I competed on all six events.

The competition was held in Norman, Oklahoma. To prepare for the meet, we put together some pretty basic routines (though they were pretty challenging to me at the time), we worked on them more and more as the competition got closer, and we finally set out for Oklahoma.

As I walked into the competition, I was overwhelmed by the size of the arena and the gymnastics environment. The arena was designed with stadium seating that descended into a pit, so I looked down on the competition area as I walked in. My heart started pumping faster and faster as I entered, and I was full of fear and excitement. In truth, it was more excitement than fear. As we walked closer to the actual competition floor, the arena seemed to become bigger and bigger, and that feeling of being overwhelmed grew more pronounced. I could see Olympic gymnast Bart Conner training on the high bar, along with many other nationally and internationally ranked gymnasts. For a twelve-year-old boy with a kid-like love for the sport of gymnastics, this went beyond the thrill of a kid in a candy store. I had never seen or experienced anything like this before, and I was not sure how to feel about seeing so many other gymnasts doing such great gymnastics. I was intimidated by seeing all of it, but that was only one of many things I thought and felt at the time.

My teammate at the time was a gymnast named Bart Padar. He and I entered the arena together, and we started stretching. Bart was not as passionate about gymnastics as I was, and he and I were not the same level, but we both trained better because of each other. We stayed close as we started warming up because we were each other's "comfort zone" in this very unfamiliar gymnastics platform. There was only a day to get used to the equipment and the atmosphere of the gym; the actual competition would not begin until the following day. Actually having one night to kind of let things sink in a little helped me to keep the emotion of the fear and excitement more on the side of excitement.

Event by event, Bart and I went around the gym warming up and doing skills from our routines that we would perform in front of crowds and judges the following day. It is good to have that warm-up time, because the equipment never feels the same at a competition as it does at "home," and it all takes some getting used to. If a floor is more or less springy, gymnasts have to make adjustments in their timing of when and how to punch and land. On pommel horse, the pommels may feel more or less slippery, and the horse might be a slightly different size, so gymnasts need to make adjustments there as well. This need to adjust is true of all the events, and this first day was our chance as gymnasts to get a feel for each event and to determine how our skills and techniques may work differently on the different equipment.

After our training session, Bart and I stayed a little longer and watched all the other gymnasts train. Like a sponge, I took in all that I saw, and it energized my mind and thoughts in many different directions. I thought about what skills I wanted to learn, I considered different techniques and better ways to do skills and combinations of skills, and I just watched in awe and excitement as other gymnasts, some of whom were incredibly skilled, did what I loved to do. If they could do those things, then I knew I had a chance to learn and do those skills, as well as new ones maybe not even seen yet.

After we had our hour-long practice, Bart and I both felt a little more calmed down. It was really exhilarating for me to meet the other gymnasts from the different clubs around the Texas and Oklahoma area. Little did I know that many of the gymnasts I met at this, my very first all-around gymnastics competition, would go on to become some of the best friends I would ever have. Not unlike any collective group of people that comes together to accomplish a mutual goal, we all had so much in common that we couldn't help but become friends and share in our passion for becoming better gymnasts. Right away, I could sense the significance of this time. On the one hand, I felt like I had found a home through this gymnastics competition, but on the other hand, this was all still very new and unfamiliar to me.

After our workout, Bart and I, along with Wayne Dixon, our coach at the time, left to get something to eat at a local restaurant and then we went back to the hotel. Knowing that I had one whole night not to worry about the competition, I was really relaxed and I enjoyed the newfound adventure for myself.

The morning came fast and as I woke up, every part of my being knew this was the day of my first all-around competition. My feelings of fear and excitement were still pretty balanced, but I could feel the balance tipping toward fear as time passed by. This was the day of competition, and on this day I knew I would go out all alone, six times, to perform my gymnastics routines. I would raise my hand to the judge and get the nod to start my routine six times, on six different pieces of equipment, with what felt to me like the whole world watching. Having no real experience with competition, I was consumed with and nearly overpowered by adrenalin and nerves. I had heard that some gymnasts got sick before their competitions as a result of nerves. I didn't get sick that day, and I can say now that I never got sick before a competition. But, that day, I felt as though I was more nervous than anybody else there.

The mind is a powerful thing, and for a twelve-year-old boy, the sky is the limit. My mind was racing that day. Bart and I started warming up just as we had done the previous day. This helped me to relax a little, as this pattern of doing gymnastics was familiar to me. As I look back, I see that throughout my career I would always look for the familiar to help me settle down before a competition. In fact, the roller coaster of emotions during an event in competition remained the same for me from this first competition on—through both Olympics and toward the end of my career. For years, there were patterns of stress and emotion, and I could count on them to be pretty consistent. Regarding my competitors, the line-up played a tremendous role in how my stress developed. When it was down to three more competitors before I competed, I remember feeling the stress build, knowing my turn was coming up. With just two more competitors, I started thinking about my routine more. When there was just one more competitor before me, my mind seemed to reach the height of activity, trying to organize all my thoughts leading up to the routine I was about to do. Then, finally, my turn would come. I would raise my hand to the judges and begin. All the fear seemed to go away when I finally got to start my routine. It was as if every emotion, training session, and thought of the competition that led up to the moment I was about to compete was put into a computer in the form of a program, and once I raised my hand to the judges, that was the equivalent of pushing the execute button. I was the computer running the program, and I just had to let it run its course. Thus, it became clear that anticipation was the biggest builder of nerves for me, so throughout my career, it was an ongoing goal of mine to keep anticipation in check.

The Oklahoma competition finally concluded. Frankly, I did better than I thought I would, weighed down with fear and nerves, but the number of mistakes I made was countless. As I completed each event throughout that first competition and throughout the many competitions to follow, I was able to relax more because I came to realize that this competition I had been so nervous about was finally taking place and really, it was not that bad. It was always the first event that was most difficult for me and for my nerves. Once the competitions started, I would get into the rhythm of the meets more and more with each event.

Over time, my goal was not to simply survive in a meet, but to excel. That is why I always preferred to start on an event I was very comfortable with, like vault, where controlling my emotions and power was not as important as it was on some of the other events, like pommel horse. There, falling off was just a slip of the hand away throughout the entire routine. That thought alone created a whole new level of nerves. But sometimes, it seemed funny to me that I would get so nervous before a meet, then I would complete the competition and feel so normal while thinking about why I had been so nervous. Recognizing this dynamic helped me to control my nerves better as my career grew.

The biggest change after completing my first all-around gymnastics meet is that I had much better grasp of what skills I wanted to work on. I also got a feel for what level the other gymnasts were—those against whom I would be competing in the years to come. This made goal setting much easier for me.

I competed in many other competitions throughout the remainder of the year. At this point of my career, I was making countless mistakes at each competition, but I was also getting better and more used to the competition environment. I was an above average talent in the world of gymnastics, but when it came to competition, I found it very difficult to be as good in front of the crowd and judges as I had been in my practice sessions. I got so nervous in competition that I made many errors, as was the case of many other gymnasts who had trouble with nerves. To this day, I believe that it is not always the best gymnast who will win a competition, but the one who can handle the pressure and perform the same way—or better—in competition as he can in training.

Although I made many mistakes when I competed, I was beginning to get recognized for my difficulty level. I was doing some very difficult skills for someone my age, and this kind of made a name for me. As one can imagine in a subjective sport, if the judges know a little bit about an athlete or have seen him or her do some good gymnastics before, they may score that athlete higher than the athlete whose name they don't recognize. So, it helped a lot to be getting some recognition.

What I lacked in competitive toughness, I made up for in difficult skill level. This allowed me to qualify for the Regional Championships, where five states in our region would come together and compete. The Regional competition was held in Arkansas. The lowest part of this experience for me was when I forgot my floor routine during the competition and started making up different tumbling passes. I was still a kid—only twelve years old—and I still just got so nervous in competitions that I could not think straight. Somehow, I made it through that rotation. The highlight of the meet overruled that embarrassment on floor; I won the high bar competition, and I took third place in the all-around. Once again, what I lacked in mental toughness and experience, I made up for in difficulty. Although I was not recognized for being a very good competitor, and although I was probably trying some skills in competition before I should have, I was establishing myself as a gymnast with potential and getting more established in the junior world of gymnastics.

Regional Championships signaled the end of that gymnastics season, and that opened up the whole summer for me to learn new skills and to grow stronger before the next competitive season started. At age thirteen, I began the season as a class two, a level that would allow me to qualify to compete in the Junior National Championships if I did well enough. The previous year, I had been a class three, and the Regional Championships were as far as a class three competitor could go. When the next season began, I started going from competition to competition. Some were good and some were bad, but I always learned something from every competition, no matter how well or how poorly I had performed. In workouts, I would try new skills, and then I would just try to make my routines cleaner and more consistent in each competition.

I really enjoyed those competitions. Not only was it nice to see my gymnastics friends and what gymnastics skills they were doing for the new season, but I also felt like I was part of something really special and unique as a gymnast. Occasionally there would be a gymnastics clinic held after a competition where an Olympian or a very established gymnast would talk to us about our gymnastics and give us insight into what might help us to get better. Olympic gymnast Bart Conner did one of these clinics, and he gave me some really good insight into things that later would help me a lot. He said in gymnastics, gymnasts should try to add their own style to the tricks they are doing because that will help set their gymnastics apart from the other gymnasts. Bart Conner was known for being a "finesse" gymnast, and his approach constantly drew the eye of the judges. He did what he did with his own style, a unique approach, and he encouraged me to do the same thing. This was an important thing to consider, because in gymnastics, many of the gymnasts do the same skills. Thus, the judges cannot help but look for not just what skills the gymnasts are doing, but for which gymnast does the skills best or in the most creative, unique way. I took Bart Conner's advice to heart, and I began to work on finding my own "finesse."

Chapter 4

MAJOR COMPETITIONS BEGIN

I think it is a priceless thing for people to have something in which they can take pride, for which they can strive, and with which they can move forward. I believe gymnastics gave me all of that, and I feel very fortunate to have been a recipient of such things. Gymnastics gave me clear direction, and at the same time it taught me what I consider to be honorable and respectable principles. Those principles also came from my parents, and since they were part of the gymnastics world in their college years, they were very understanding and supportive of me and of my accomplishments in gymnastics. They often said, "We are proud of whatever you do in the sport. This is your time, not ours, so keep enjoying it and do the best you can." I will always be grateful for their support and their encouragement.

It was with my parents' support, and with all the gifts that gymnastics seemed to be handing to me, that I moved forward in the sport I loved. As my gymnastics progressed, I became more aware of the judges and the scores I was receiving. I began to compare my scores in every competition to scores I had received before, and I would determine if the scores and my performances were getting better or worse. This was often frustrating, however, because some judges were more strict and issued lower scores compared to other judges, and as we were judged by different judges at each competition, it was difficult to find consistency and clear cut areas to work on.

Naturally, I was not the only gymnast frustrated by the scoring system. The subjectivity of gymnastics judging gets a lot of attention in the competitive sports world, and it's easy to see why. In baseball, when the ball flies all the way out of the park, that is pretty black-and-white—it's a home run. In gymnastics, there are human beings judging other human beings who are displaying a form of art, so there is subjectivity. Sometimes, it is funny—often ridiculous. I remember that when I competed in Germany, for instance, the Germans always scored higher than they should have. Germany was kind of known for being more excessive in this political bias. But, no matter what country I competed in, the athletes from that country scored well. The United States was no exception; when I competed at an international meet in the United States, the U.S. gymnasts scored a little higher than normal. Although fundamentally this is not right, I guess there is a certain justice to the judging in the big picture.

Anyway, after getting more recognition in the international world of gymnastics, I saw my scores start to get higher because I was more established. Even before I got on an event, the judge might have had a favorable opinion of my capabilities or of my routine, based on the last competition in which he saw me or based on what he might have heard in the gymnastics community. Because of that, after competing for a while, I stopped caring if I scored higher or lower, as long as I was ranked fairly among the other gymnasts. For instance, if I knew I was the best gymnast on an event, I did not care if I got a 10 or an 8 as long as I was ranked fairly and as long as the scores were correct in placing the best gymnast in first place. So, over time, I concentrated less on what score I received and more on what gymnast would beat me—or what gymnast I would beat—because we were all subject to the same judges. If we were being ranked properly, that is all I really cared about.

My competitive season as a class two continued, and I learned to be consistent enough and to compete well enough to qualify for the Junior National Championships, to be held in Eugene, Oregon. As I prepared for that meet, I knew my problem in gymnastics remained the same: I was not hindered by my skill level, but by my ability to successfully compete my routines in competition while under pressure. Finding the balance between doing the most difficult skills I could do and not having any mistakes while I did them became my goal, and I desired to practice with that in mind. But then, a new problem arose. A couple of weeks before the Junior National competition, the gym where I was training closed down while another gym was being built, so I had no gym in which to prepare for the competition. As crazy as it might sound, we actually put the gymnastics equipment at my parents' house, and I practiced in the back yard and in the living room. I guess my poor mom never had a true living room! We had the pommel horse in the living room, and I trained my routines surrounded by couches, a TV, and all the other furniture that makes up a typical living room. In the gym, I used chalk (white powder) to keep my hands dry while working out on the pommel horse, and this did not change even while I worked out at home. As you might imagine, chalk got all over the living room. That isn't all. My feet hit the ceiling when I swung up to do my handstand dismount. The whole room was my playground. Fortunately, the parallel bars were in the back yard. Though that saved the living room a little bit, it was tricky to get them even on the grass so I could train properly.

Looking back, I can really see how incredibly supportive my parents were. And thinking about it now, after all the competitions I have been in and knowing what true training requires before a competition, this was about as crazy as it could get. My coach and parents did everything they possibly could so I could at least have some training before the meet. We could not set up the other equipment in the house or yard, so I had to wait until we got to the meet to train on those events again.

After arriving in Eugene for the Junior National Championships, I had a couple of days before the meet to train in the competition arena. That helped a great deal to get used to the equipment on which I had not been able to train back home. My competition was fierce; I was to compete against the best male gymnasts age fifteen and under in the U.S., and most of them had not been training in their living rooms. Keep in mind, though, that all of these gymnasts, no matter how talented, were very young. As a result, a lot of mistakes were made. I saw a gymnast land straight on top of the high bar during a dismount. I saw a gymnastics ring break in half as the gymnast did his swing for his dismount. That was not the gymnast's fault, though, and the chances of such a thing are probably one in a million. At the junior level, nobody is really all that experienced, but I saw many gymnasts doing incredible skills, and I learned a lot about the level of gymnastics being performed throughout the country in the junior division.

The day of the meet, we all had an hour to warm up our routines before the competition started. In warm-ups, I was really feeling comfortable, and my routines were pretty solid. In the actual competition, though, I pretty much fell apart. It was the same old story—I could not seem to display in competition the routines I had mastered in practice (albeit practice in my living room). For instance, as I walked up to compete on floor, I actually tripped on the floor exercise carpet as I started my routine. I didn't fall, but I lost some points and some pride. Then, in the middle of my routine, I was supposed to slide my body up to a handstand from a push-up position, and instead of pressing to a handstand, I fell down to a headstand. It was a pretty bad start, and the rest of the competition pretty much followed in the same way. I did have some bright moments—like vault, where I completed my *Tsukahara* (a half front flip with a half twist to my hands onto the vault, with one and a half flips backwards to my feet) just like I had done in practice—but they were not really bright enough to erase the multitude of dark moments. Sometimes I made mistakes because I was nervous. Sometimes I made mistakes because I was not properly prepared. And sometimes, no matter how well the stars are aligned, a person just has a bad meet. To this day, I am not sure which one of these was my main problem, but I suppose that training in the living room and back yard did make it a challenge to be prepared the way I should have been for a competition of this level, or of any level, for that matter.

With my first national competition behind me, I finished the summer of '83 motivated and with my head full of grand ideas of what skills I wanted to learn, having seen all the great gymnastics at Nationals. I began training at a new gym, *TGSA*, so the limitations of my living room furniture and low ceiling were lifted. Once again, I felt like a kid in a candy store. It was a very good time for me. Really, summer is a good time for all gymnasts because they don't have to spend all their time on training routines; they can also concentrate on trying new things and learning new skills. For me, this was like the ultimate playtime, and I learned skill after skill. As summer wound down, my coaches and I had to decide what new skills to put into my routines, and together we had to determine if those skills would be ready for competition or not.

Because of the improvements I had made in the previous years, by January of 1984, I was invited to the Olympic Training Center in Colorado Springs to take part in what was simply called National Team Testing. This happened every January right after Christmas, before the new competition year started. Gymnasts from all around the country would travel to the Olympic Training Center and be tested to see if they could successfully complete a long list of very difficult skills. If they completed all the skills, they were placed on the Junior National team, which consisted of the top ten boys in the country in gymnastics in their respective age groups, all age eighteen or under.

In the testing, we were required to complete between six and twelve skills for each event, and we were judged from one to ten on how well we did these skills. If we could not do a skill, we received a "fail" on that skill. With more than one "fail," a gymnast could not make the Junior National team. One gymnast after another mounted the event and had three tries to do the required skill.

Now, in a typical meet, gymnasts add up all their individual scores to make a team score. But, while we are out competing, we are on the event all by ourselves, earning an individual score, and it is a very individual thing. That is not to say that there is not camaraderie in our sport, but in actual competition, we rely completely on ourselves and how we have trained. This "individual moment" became more magnified than ever before as I competed for a spot on the Junior National team. Never had I felt more alone. I had a couple of skills that were very challenging for me, such as completing five press handstands (slowly lifting my body from the ground into a handstand position without swinging). I was a very agile and acrobatic gymnast, but I was not that physically strong for a gymnast at that time. Somehow, though, I did manage to power through the five presses and pass. But, although I succeeded in completing my presses, there was one trick on the high bar I could not complete. Because of this one trick, I did not make the Junior National team. The skill was a *Stalder*. It is executed by swinging around the bar in a handstand position, then bringing the body close to the bar while straddling the legs, putting them behind the ears, and swinging all the way around back to a handstand. I was flexible enough to do this trick, but I simply could not figure out the correct technique.

I was frustrated by not making the Junior National team, though honestly, I was not really expected to. In the long run, I think the disappointment motivated me more to learn better skills than the skills I had seen the other guys doing. When I got back home, I not only figured out the Stalder, I also became hungrier and more motivated than ever to learn more, to prove my gymnastics ability, and to show what I could do. My motivation was based on something that holds true for gymnasts of any age and any level. Even the youngest children in gymnastics find motivation when they are taught a new trick and when they learn to do it well. They become eager to learn another trick, and then another one, and so on. It is really very simple motivation.

By the time the competitive season began, I was much improved from the previous year, and I was more recognized since I had participated in the testing in Colorado. Thus, I had a much better competitive year than I had had previously. I made fewer mistakes in competition, and I got better and better at handling the pressure. I was also doing a very difficult skill on floor exercise by this time. It was a back flip in the straight body position with three twists—a triple full. Not many world-class gymnasts were performing this skill at the time, so for me to be so young and to be doing this trick was a great way for me to catch the judges' attention. Actually, I was able to complete this skill successfully only about fifty percent of the time, but hit or miss, it gave me a credible reputation as a gymnast with increasing talent.

Once again, the competitive season came to a climax with the Junior National Championships that were to be held in Albuquerque, New Mexico. If I finished in the top ten in the all-around, I would be named to the 1984 Junior National team. That was my goal.

The competition went very well for me, though it was not perfect. Highs and lows. The highlights were on high bar and floor exercise. On the high bar, on the first day of the two-day competition, I scored a 9.9—only one-tenth away from a perfect 10! That brought a lot of attention my way. Then, on floor, I succeeded in completing the triple full, and I became the Junior National Champion on floor exercise. The low point was that I had a major mistake on the event that would ultimately become my nemesis— the pommel horse. That mistake cost me a spot on the Junior National team, because even with my success on high bar and floor exercise, I finished in twelfth place, two places behind the team requirement.

After I experienced many ups and downs in competition, I began to notice a pattern that would follow those meets. After a bad meet, I would feel discouraged for about two days. Then, after I began training again in the gym, I would begin to feel the motivation building, and I would transfer that negativity into hard work. It wasn't an easy task, because when I say I would feel discouraged, I mean I felt deathlike. Not to be too dramatic, but when I trained and hoped so much for success, it was devastating when the result was quite the opposite. I was a very emotional competitor, and I felt nerves and failure and disappointment all in a very potent way. Success was equally potent. When I would win a meet, I was euphoric, and I felt like I was on top of the world. It was as if every piece of my life had been put snugly into place, fitting perfectly.

Looking back, and recognizing that this happens pretty naturally and regularly, I see how dangerous the dynamic can be when one's self-esteem is dictated by one thing. My one thing, of course, was gymnastics. When I was doing well in gymnastics, I felt great in my life. When I was doing poorly, I felt really bad in my life. Because of my experiences with gymnastics and with the way it affected me, I now feel very strongly about everyone keeping a balance with everything in life. This balance is important in how we see ourselves, how we interact with people, and how we approach achieving a goal. Maintaining this balance is a skill within itself, and it should be taught and nurtured in athletes from a very young age.

For me, I eventually did find a way to balance it all. The balance became like food for me—my sustenance—because my positive feelings after a good competition lasted much longer than my negative feelings after a bad competition. Keep in mind, gymnastics was my one true passion. I could not get enough of it, so my balance came mostly in adjusting my mindset and finding ways to control the nerves, the negative thoughts, and the reaction to pressure. It is true that those not in the gymnastics world might see high level gymnastics as too much work and requiring too much dedication. That is not entirely off base. But, when people love doing something so much, and when that thing is so fulfilling and challenging, it rarely crosses their minds that it is "work." It is a gratifying challenge, with no time limit to succeed. I never felt I sacrificed anything, and I would never have wanted to be on a different path. I believe we all take different paths in life, and those paths lead us in different directions. I don't categorize those different directions as being better or worse than others, just different. No matter what direction we choose, we can make it work, we can learn, and we can find gratification.

Chapter 5

CHANGES AND TRIALS

While I was training, if someone had given me a billion dollars and offered me the chance to do anything I wanted in the world, I would have said I was already doing it. It was gymnastics. I couldn't have imagined investing my time and energy into anything else. It consumed not only my time and energy, but also my thoughts, my dreams—my everything. It was blissful, and I wouldn't have had it any other way. There was so much value in it—not solely for the sport, but for every part of life. My best friends were also gymnasts, and they were good and respectable people. We all had empathy for each other and for what we were trying to do as athletes. We were developing a work ethic, setting priorities and goals, learning respect, compassion, honor, and discipline, and discovering how to fail and how to succeed. Those things carried over into life after competition, and I take pleasure in knowing that it was from gymnastics that I learned about those things.

It's important to note that being the best athlete in the world does not make someone the best person in the world. The two aren't necessarily connected; in fact, they can be mutually exclusive. People need to pay attention, and they need to absorb all that can be learned in such an intense lifestyle. Character is important, and if the quest for success outweighs the development and integrity of character, I believe it is only a matter of time before major conflict will emerge. I think these conflicts arise when the passion dies, or when there is no balance between character and success. People need to truly love doing what they are doing. That applies not just to sports; I believe people should make a living doing what they are passionate about. Of course, that is not always possible. If it is not, people should find an alternative—a simple job that will pay the bills—and still find a way to pursue what they are passionate about outside of work. When people are plugged in to their passion, they are much happier. And, when people do something that brings out the best in them in all aspects, they, the people around them, and the world around them are affected in a better and more positive way.

For me, my passion carried me forward, into 1985. Once again, it was back to the gym to prepare for the next season. Junior National Testing came quickly, and I headed back to the Olympic Training Center in Colorado to try to pass all the skills and qualify for the Junior National team. I had improved a great deal over the summer, and this time, I qualified easily. The skill that I had not been able to do the previous year had become easy for me.

Once I was on the Junior team, I was invited to training camps around the country to learn new techniques, to train with the other National team members (it is very important to train with athletes who are equal or better in order to be motivated and challenged to reach for the next level), and to see what the new trends were—all at the expense of the USGF (the *United States Gymnastic Federation*, which is now operating under the name *U.S.A. Gymnastics, or USAG*). In addition, being on the Junior team meant that I had a chance of being selected to go overseas to compete in order to gain some international experience. It is important to note that once the judging world knew a gymnast was on the Junior National team, there was the political advantage of being recognized.

At one of these gymnastics camps at the Olympic Training Center, I actually had my first international competition as a junior. It was against the Italian Junior National team. This was a great honor for me, especially because I was only fourteen years old. I had a really good competition, but I was still very young and inexperienced, so I was not really in medal contention. Even so, I was able to see what the Italians were doing with their gymnastics and observe which techniques they were using for certain skills. It was another eye-opener for me to see what direction I wanted to go, and this time it was much more within my grasp to reach the level of gymnastics I saw compared to when I was twelve.

The season moved along with many meets. I was becoming smarter, more experienced, and more consistent as a competitor. Rather than perform all of my difficult skills in each set, I would take out the most inconsistent and difficult skills if they were giving me trouble in order to approach a competition with more confidence.

Confidence is a priceless asset in competition. Some people are born with it, and others have to build it. I had to build it. I found my greatest motivation in the fear of failure. I hated that feeling, so I trained harder so I could avoid it. Others are motivated by the chance to show the skill level they have and to meet with success. The two seem very different, but the end result can be the same: accomplishing higher levels and reaching higher goals.

Junior Nationals once again came upon me, and this time, I had a shot at winning. The competition was held in Ohio. I competed well, and I took second in the all-around. I also finished very high on many of the individual events. The significance of this competition was that I was chosen, along with one other gymnast, to travel overseas to Hungary to compete in my first international meet away from the United States. There were more than ten countries in the competition, and although it was for kids under the age of sixteen (I had just turned fifteen), I was able to see the level and trends of gymnastics being done around the world. I saw what level I would have to achieve in order to be world class and internationally competitive. I placed second at this competition, which was much better than I expected. It was a good competition, and I felt good that I had added more difficulty for this event and come through without failure.

After returning home from Hungary, I started to feel more like I could achieve the level of gymnastics that was being done around the world—maybe even a little better! Hope and looking to the future were the driving forces at this time of my career. Everyone needs hope and goals; without them, they just won't improve, and they might give up. It's sad to consider how many things have not been accomplished because people have given up too soon.

I was sixteen years old when the next season started. Because I was already on the Junior National team, I did not have to go to testing that year. My coach and I decided that I would try to compete with the senior gymnasts at the U.S. National Championships instead of competing as a junior. I was still young enough to compete at the Junior Nationals, but we felt like it would be good to see how I would do against the best gymnasts in the country, regardless of age.

Competing with the seniors meant that I would have to do the Olympic compulsories on the first day of Nationals—routines that all the elite athletes had to do on all six events. The routines were the same for everybody and designed to strengthen basics. They also allowed for a more objective score from the judges. The second day would be the optionals, which were routines that a coach and gymnast put together, made up of the most difficult skills a gymnast could do. (Incidentally, in today's world of gymnastics, high-level compulsories no longer exist. High level competitions are based solely on optionals—the most difficult routines an individual gymnast can train and perform.) The compulsories were challenging to me; I was much better at optionals. But, I would have to compete in both, and after the competition, the scores would be combined from the compulsories and the optionals, and that total score would lead to the ranking of the competitors.

On the first day, the day of the compulsories, I had a really bad day. I had trained pretty well for the competition as far as I knew, but I made many more mistakes than I thought I would. The second day, I did much better, but I think I had lost a lot of confidence from the previous day's performance. I finished fifty-ninth in the U.S. That was not good for a gymnast at my level. Although I was a junior, I felt as if I should have been able to do well enough to finish in the top twenty-five. It was discouraging, but it was motivating at the same time.

After Nationals, I learned that the gym where I was training was going to be taken over by new management and would no longer have a team program. This was a major downer for me, because it meant that I would have no gym in which to train anymore. My mom and dad wanted me to be able to continue in gymnastics, of course, so we all started thinking about what could be done. My dad was a manager of a retail store at the time, and he was very good at what he did. Even though he was quite established, he was hoping for advancement, so he was open to changing jobs. He interviewed with a company that offered him the advancement he desired. There were three cities to which he could choose to relocate, and one was Albuquerque, New Mexico. We were familiar with a gym called *Gold Cup* in Albuquerque that was known for having an excellent men's gymnastics program. Mom and Dad had been through New Mexico for vacations and really liked that part of the country, so a move to Albuquerque was pretty appealing to them. Even my brother, Joe, did not mind; he was tired of Texas and he welcomed a change. So, in the summer of 1986, we decided to move the family to Albuquerque.

For such a life-changing event, the move went pretty smoothly. We quickly got settled in New Mexico, discovering right away that it could get very hot in the summertime. Even so, it was great weather for training. It wasn't humid, which was what I was used to. It was a "dry heat," as they say. Better, I guess. Not as draining, though it took some getting used to. The altitude was also kind of a shock, but it was a great way to enhance endurance.

I immediately began training at Gold Cup Gymnastics. The owner and head coach of the gym was Ed Burch, a man I had seen and with whom I had trained at many Junior gymnastics camps. Burch was the consummate "slave driver" with a critical eye. The assistant coach was Bill Foster. Bill was the technical expert of how skills should be learned and practiced, and he knew the judging rules very well.

When I arrived at Gold Cup, I was known as a mediocre competitor but a very talented gymnast, and Burch liked that a lot. He was a very good coach and a great trainer. Little did I realize that when I joined Gold Cup, my gymnastics would be totally revolutionized. After the first day of training, I was sore, and not long into my new training regimen, I realized that I had not really been training hard at all in Texas. The workouts at Gold Cup were much more organized and demanding. Each day, our workouts were posted on a bulletin board with all of the skills, routines, stretches and strength we were required to do, and Burch would not accept anything less than our very best at every workout.

The team I started training with was made up of many gymnasts against whom I had competed at various meets around the country, and they challenged me and pushed me more than I had ever been challenged or pushed before. They were very strong gymnasts. The best of them was Chainey Umphrey, who would later make the '96 Olympic team. Chainey was known for being a great tumbler and for having an incredibly muscular—if not bulky—type body, like a linebacker. Another teammate, Trent Dimas, would later make the '92 Olympic team and bring home an Olympic gold medal on high bar. Trent was known for having great style and really nice body positions. Ted Dimas, Trent's older brother, was known for being very physically strong. Brad Bryan was the cleanest gymnast in form and execution. There were other gymnasts on the team, but these were the best guys and were either on the Junior National team or had been at one time or another. They all knew me from the gymnastics circle, but at first they did not really know how to accept me into their world. They had been at Gold Cup for years, and I was the new kid. Of course, we all respected each other, but even with mutual respect, there is a need to earn one's place in a gym.

Burch spent a lot of time with me in the first few weeks, and that helped me to feel more at home—like I belonged there. He saw many things he wanted to change, and he had a good feel for the direction in which he wanted me to work. I was learning so much and improving so fast just in the first few weeks that I was blown away. I had never trained that hard before. As I think about our team, I remember that we were still young, and only a very few of us were secure. It did cause the team to work much harder and helped me to fit in as we competed against each other in the gym. Burch was really good about pitting his athletes against each other to push for improvement. He liked it when we pushed ourselves to be better than the other guy. Although it was a little stressful sometimes, it worked, and we all did get better.

I can still remember how "different" the system at Gold Cup seemed when I arrived. It was truly an adjustment for me. Most of my friends back in Texas had been a little more easy-going than the Gold Cup team. Gold Cup gymnasts were very aggressive and competitive. They were passionate about becoming the best, and they saw other gymnasts that were improving fast as both a challenge and a threat. That attitude and dynamic, I believe, was one of the biggest assets of Gold Cup, along with Burch being very demanding of his athletes and a very good trainer. Each day I looked at the workout posted on the board and was shocked by how much was there—how much was required. Workouts were very intense, and we did a lot of routines. I had been used to working a lot more skills, but these guys did full routines each and every day. That is what made them so consistent in meets. Gold Cup was known for having gymnasts in great shape—better shape than anyone else in the country. After only being there a short time, I could easily see why.

Eventually I became an accepted team member at Gold Cup, and before long, Albuquerque felt like home. Mom and I moved out to Albuquerque about six months before Dad and my brother moved because Dad had to take care of the sale of the house and finish his orientation and training with his new job. We rented a small townhouse fairly close to the gym, and I registered to be a junior at La Cueva High School in the fall. Once school began, my day consisted of getting up, having Mom drive me to school, having Mom pick me up from school, watching about thirty minutes of TV, then going to the gym. Mom was a great chauffeur. I trained for about three hours each day, six days a week. Mom would pick me up from the gym, and we would have a late dinner, watch M*A*S*H on TV, then go to sleep. We would wake up to the same routine the next day.

I improved more at this time than at any other time in my career. It would show throughout the upcoming season. Because we did so many more routines in training than I was used to, I started making fewer mistakes in competition and my scores began to rise dramatically. I was improving on all levels: strength, flexibility, and mental toughness. Each day in the gym played out as a small competition, for we would evaluate who could have the best workout and do skills the best. It helped all of us to progress and to grow more confident.

Once again, the year ended with National Championships. And, once again, the best gymnasts in the country would be there. We were now competing as seniors, so age would not be a factor. Three of us from Gold Cup qualified to take part. We all did pretty well. As for me, I had a great competition and finished in twenty-fourth place. This was a major jump from the previous year's finish of fifty-ninth. Also, it was one year before the Olympics, so a good finish was pretty significant. Although I had never thought of the Olympic team being a reality at this point, my coach had, and he set out to get not just me but any of his gymnasts on the team. I guess the approaching Olympics should have been my goal, but we were still so much younger than the Senior National team members that I did not really think about it. I thought maybe five years later, when I was twenty-two, I might have a chance to make an Olympic team. But Burch had more immediate goals; he was determined to shoot for the 1988 Olympic team. I just agreed to work hard and never really thought that much about it. Besides, I was still only twenty-fourth in the country, and athletes had to be in the top seven to make the Olympic team.

Because I did so well at Nationals, I qualified to take part in the U.S. Olympic Festival in the summer of 1987. The Olympic Festival is kind of like a little national Olympics, and several sports send their best athletes to compete. The Olympic Festival did not qualify a gymnast for anything, but it was televised and a great opportunity to get more experience and more exposure in the sport. The best gymnasts were always at the Olympic Festival, so it was a great chance to measure one gymnast's abilities against another's.

At the Olympic Festival, we only had to do the optional routines. This was great for me, because optionals include the more impressive gymnastics, and as I mentioned, I was much stronger in optionals than I was in compulsories. I had one of the best competitions of my life and finished third in the all-around. This was a milestone for me and the first time I sincerely thought I might have an outside chance at the Olympic team in 1988. In order to make the team, though, I knew I would have to become stronger in my compulsories. So, I returned to my gym to train, my thoughts focused on this new goal.

The U.S. gymnastics world chose to do something different the year of the 1988 Olympics. They held National Championships in the winter as well as in the summer. This was new, and it was probably put in place as a way to see how the United States' top gymnasts were doing at the beginning of an Olympic year. Winter Nationals took place in Omaha, Nebraska. Most athletes were not in their best shape at that time because it was held early in the competitive year. My coach saw it as an opportunity to excel and to show everybody that I was a contender for the Olympic team, regardless of my age. I was seventeen, and even though I would be eighteen for the Olympics, I was still younger than the average male gymnast who had a shot at the Olympic team. When we went to Winter Nationals, I was in very good shape. My goal was to finish in the top eighteen, because that would qualify me to be on the Senior National team. If I qualified for that, it would help my chances to then make the Olympic team—still only an outside chance at that time. I finished in the eighteenth spot, barely sneaking in there to qualify for the team. But, it did not matter by what margin I qualified. I was on the team.

Higher level gymnastics naturally meant more intense training, and Burch was never one to let his athletes slow down. A typical day of training for me involved going to the gym at seven o'clock a.m. and doing about one hour of strength before going to school. After school, I would go home for an hour and then head back to the gym. I had gone to high school for two years in Texas before moving to New Mexico, and I had more credits from my Texas school than I needed to graduate from my New Mexico school. This worked out really well for me, because it allowed me to go to school one hour later than normal and leave two hours early, so I could train more. Because of the high intensity of training, I was in better shape than I had ever been in before. In fact, after awhile, it seemed that no matter how long I trained, I did not get tired anymore. All I did was train, go to four classes of school each day, eat, and sleep. It was my life, it made perfect sense, and I could not have imagined anything else.

Training led to competitions, and each competition went by until it was finally time to go to National Championships in the summer of 1988. The way it worked back then was that the top eighteen gymnasts from the National Championships would qualify to compete at the Olympic Trials. Then, the top seven athletes from the Trials would be named to the Olympic team. This meant that with Nationals and Trials, I would have to have the two best competitions of my life, under more pressure than I had ever been under before. With school out for the summer, I was able to train for these competitions with two full workouts each day. I did about two to three hours in the morning on the first three events and two to three hours in the afternoon on the last three events. My new training regimen at Gold Cup had helped me very much and I was a really good competitor at this point, but every athlete knows that anything can happen in competition. I knew that a slip of the hand or a misplaced foot could mean that I would not be on the Olympic team. But, I trained my hardest, and I went to Nationals to prove what I could do.

Being at Nationals was an experience I will never forget. The intensity of it, since it was leading to an Olympic team, was unbelievable. I was confident that I had trained well, and event after event, I hit my routines, so I got even more confident as the competition went on. As intense as the meet was, I was having a great time because I was so much better prepared for it than I had ever been for any other meet. No matter how I would place in the end, I felt like it was a success, because I knew it would be the best finish I had ever had. I was young—only eighteen—and I think I was moving through the experience kind of like a chicken with my head cut off. I did not know how I was supposed to feel, so my naiveté and my excitement helped me to relax more than the other gymnastics veterans. There was very little expectation for me, other than that which I placed on myself (which would always be more than anybody else could put on me), but it was not magnified by being expected to make the Olympic team. So, I just tried to enjoy the experience and make the most of my time. Even so, of course the first goal and priority was to qualify for the Olympic Trials.

My competition was fierce. In an Olympic year, all the gymnasts are generally in the best shape of their lives, so it is the most competitive year of the four-year cycle. I had an incredible meet, and after all twelve routines were complete, I finished in sixth place. This was a shocker for the gymnastics world, for me, and even for my coach, who had always felt as if the sky was the limit. Everything worked out exactly the way Burch and I had hoped, and that was not easy to do in this sport. Burch and I knew then that if I could have the same competition at the Trials that I had just had at Nationals, I would definitely make the Olympic team. That realization made me more serious than I had ever been before, because the dream of becoming an Olympian was actually within my reach.

After Nationals, Burch and I returned to Albuquerque with a lot of momentum. We knew we had a training regimen that was really working for me, so we just continued training the same way for the Olympic Trials. I had about three weeks to train before Trials, and I used those weeks to maintain the shape I was in for the Championships. Training was really made up of doing my routines over and over. We still did strength and stretch, but at that point it was all about perfecting the routines I would be competing.

Olympic Trials were held in Salt Lake City, Utah. I knew most of the other gymnasts that were taking part. Some were intense, and others were more laid back. When I was in the gym, I was much more intense about my gymnastics, but at the competition, I was surprisingly laid back and still enjoying the ride of just being there.

The Trials brought a lot of attention. It was a huge event for us, for the city, and really, for the nation. There was a lot of media attention, and there was a lot of speculation from the media about what the outcome would be. For two days before the meet, training went well, and I felt mentally ready. The first day was the compulsory competition, and I hit all my routines. After that first day, I was in seventh place, which kept me in contention for the Olympic team. The optional competition was to take place the following day. Though I had come in with a laid back feeling, optionals were approaching, and I could not keep from calculating scores and running "what if" scenarios in my head. Once the pressure hits, it is a difficult thing to force oneself to relax. I learned to calm down in steps, and eventually, I was able to control my nerves much better. I was still very excited just to be a part of this huge experience, but I really did want to make the team, more than anything I had ever wanted before.

In the optionals competition, I began on pommel horse. This was one of my weaker events. In training it had often been one of my better events, but there was a lot of room for error. I would think "one slip of the hand, I fall", then I would get nervous and make mistakes. I would have preferred to compete on pommel horse later in the meet, after I had become more comfortable, but I had no choice. I started the event and just as I had done hundreds of times in practice, I nailed my set! This was a huge start for me. My most problematic event—my nemesis—was behind me. After pommel horse, I was off to a stronger event for me, the rings, where I hit another great routine. Next was floor, and I did an above average set, sticking my dismount solid. Parallel bars were next, and although it was a good event for me, it was easier to get out of control while swinging between the bars. No problem, though. I hit another good routine. The announcer called out the results after each rotation, but I tried not to pay too much attention as I had two more events to compete. High bar was next, and it had the potential to be my best event. I was doing a risky sequence of three releases—a pretty unique thing to do. In fact, I was the only one in the United States doing that at the time. The bonus points were very high, but so was the risk. I knew that after high bar, I had only a vault to complete, and vault was one of my most solid and consistent events. In my mind, it all came down to this high bar set. I mounted the bar as my coach stood under it as a safety precaution. The first release was perfect and set up the second release very well. I went straight into the next release, then right into the third. I had made my most difficult sequence, so I only had to finish with my double back flip in the layout position with two twists, which was one of the most difficult dismounts on high bar being done in the world. I was the only one in the meet doing this dismount, and I needed to do it well. This day was no different from a day in practice, and I landed with only a small hop. My coach jumped into the air, elated.

With that success on high bar, we both knew how close I was to making the Olympic team. It was completely surreal. I was in fifth place after high bar, and all I had to do was vault over the vaulting horse and land on my feet, and I would be on the team. I started running down the eighty-foot runway and launched my vault, and my heart pounded when I completed it well, as I had done so many times before in practice. My coach gave me a huge bear hug to celebrate, because we both knew I had just made the Olympic team.

Finishing well—completing that vault successfully—was truly one of the greatest moments in my life. After all the competitors finished, the scores were tallied and the officials called out the top athletes. My name came fifth, and I was called out as an Olympic team member. Hearing my name that day is something I will never forget. In truth, there is no way to describe that feeling of being named to the Olympic team. The euphoria, the ecstasy— it was truly overwhelming. And, that was just the beginning. After Trials, I returned home to a large crowd of friends and fellow gymnasts at the airport. The media was there, and I really was surprised by all the attention. I guess that's because it still hadn't quite sunk in for me. I was unprepared to see how many other people were affected in a positive way, but I loved being part of something so huge and so exciting. Everybody who was part of my life was now part of the bigger-than-life event known as the Olympics. We were all elevated, and it was amazing.

As great as those first experiences were, and as indescribable as that moment was when I knew I had made the team, it was only in the years following the Olympics that I learned what it truly meant to be an Olympian. I have now come to understand that making it to the Olympics is a pinnacle in life, and to have reached that felt bigger than life. People—strangers—approached me for years after the Olympics as if they knew me, and they asked questions or told how they watched me compete and were excited to see me do well. It was as if they knew how much hard work I had put into this and they were excited to see me succeed. In a way it felt like we were all in it together, which is the main reason I have been genuinely proud to represent our country. Even now, decades later in my life, people respond to me in that same way. An Olympian is an Olympian is an Olympian, and that is a priceless thing.

Chapter 6

1988 OLYMPICS IN SEOUL, KOREA

When I made the Olympic team in 1988, I had no idea what was ahead of me. With each new day, I was again shocked at how much attention the Olympics brought. I was amazed at the time how many people were touched and affected by the Olympics, and by my place on the team. It was kind of a ripple effect. When I made the team, there were newspaper articles about me in many of the towns in which I had once lived, even though I had not lived there for years. My grandmother in Chicago had friends she had not heard from for a long time call her out of the blue to say they heard her grandson had made the Olympic team and to offer her congratulations. A small town newspaper in Iowa reported my position on the Olympic team and listed the excitement of around thirty relatives of mine that I had never even met. We were all lifted up by that great moment of accomplishment— by the realization of a dream—and again, it felt like we were all in it together. We had all imagined it, but to actually experience it, and to be part of it, was absolutely surreal.

I was blown away by the initial excitement, but I quickly realized that the Olympic Games stand as a bigger life event than I had ever expected. I also realized that in many ways, the Olympic Trials were more pressure-filled than the Olympics because if athletes have a bad day at Trials, they don't make the team. Once they make the Olympic team, they can go all out and hunt for medals. My hunt could not begin unless my training intensified, but I knew that no matter what, no one could take away my already life-changing experience.

Once I made the team, the next step in my experience was to travel to Indianapolis, where the team had a three-week training camp together before going over to Seoul, Korea, where the 1988 Olympics were held. We all came together in Indianapolis and stayed at a nice hotel. I knew the other gymnasts who had made the Olympic team pretty well, and even though I was much younger than they were, they accepted me as one of them.

For three weeks, we trained twice a day, putting in three hours in the morning and three hours in the afternoon. Our workouts were intense, filled with energy, and surrounded by media interviews and other activities. I thought there had been a lot of media for the Olympic Trials, but the interest and the coverage only increased from that point forward. It was huge. Everybody wanted to interview us and to know about how things were going and how we felt. It was overwhelming at times; I think the team members themselves were still trying to figure everything out, and knowing how we felt and how others felt was part of the intensity. It was very hard to put it all into words.

Despite the intensity, and maybe partly because of it, the training camp went well for all of us. We were all pretty healthy and in great shape. We were a young and new team. The gymnasts from the 1984 Olympic Gold Medal team had all retired except for Scott Johnson, and he was part of our team. Since the veterans were mostly gone, the U.S. was in a rebuilding stage. To get a medal as a team was considered very improbable. We just wanted to make a good showing and to see what happened.

From the Indianapolis camp we flew to L.A. to go through what is called "processing." There, we met up with all the U.S. Olympic athletes from all the different sports, and we got all our Olympic apparel, supplies, and gifts provided by the Olympic sponsors. Since it was the Olympics, there were many sponsors who gave things to the athletes. We received cameras, sunglasses, cologne, toothpaste, suits, socks, watches, etc. It was an incredible experience. We all walked through a warehouse going from station to station, getting fitted for clothes and other accessories. It was great. We could have gone to Seoul with nothing and still been able to live for a month with all that we received.

After processing in Los Angeles, we flew to Korea. Because we were the Olympic team, we got to fly first class. That really helped with such a long flight. Once we landed, we went straight to register in order to get our credentials to enter the Olympic village and competition venue. It was the middle of the night, but everybody was still up and excited. We got to our apartment where there was an upstairs and downstairs, and it was really nice. They put two athletes in each room. My roommate was Dominick Minicucci, another gymnast on the U.S. team who was one year older than I was. We had become good friends, and we were roommates for the entire Olympics.

Athletes competing in diving, tae kwon do, and a couple of other sports were also in our building. It was all very exciting to me, and we were really spoiled. Everything in the village was free, such as soda, energy drinks, and food. They also offered free video games. Everything was done so well that I could barely take it all in. Walking around the village, we got to rub shoulders with and meet the best athletes in the world in all different kinds of sports. It was such a great experience. Everyone there was a life-long athlete and shared in that passion for each respective sport, so we had an instant bond. Even if we did not share the sport, we shared the dream, the journey, the work, and once we were there, the amazing reality.

A typical day at the Olympics was to wake up, have breakfast, and go to the arena for training. Just as it was in my early days of competitions, we went from event to event, getting used

to the slightly different equipment and fine-tuning our more difficult skills. Gymnastics was going to be one of the first sports to
be competed in the Seoul Olympics, so we did not have much time
to train before the Games started. We trained our hardest, and we
watched the other countries as they trained as well. We recognized
the talents of our competition, and seeing them there brought out
our competitive side, of course, but it also inspired us because we
respected the athletes and the sport so highly.

Because I was extremely passionate about gymnastics, I had the
ability to remember and recall the history and routines of most of
the athletes taking part in the Olympics from all twelve countries
represented. (In the Olympics, only the top twelve countries in the
world qualify to participate in competition). The fact that I was
there training and competing with gymnasts that I had grown up
admiring and trying to be like had a big impact on me. Many of
the gymnasts I admired the most were on the Soviet team, and they
were dominant in gymnastics at the time. It's strange to think how
time changes things; that was the last time they competed as the
Soviet Union.

Everyone was nice at the Olympics, but they were also very
focused. That included the media. During training, we could see
camera men lined up outside the barrier of the gym snapping pictures. They would be there all day long. It was a media circus, but
still, in the training session, there was a bit of a laid back feeling

After our morning training session, we would go back to the
village for lunch. During that mid-day break, we walked around
or just chilled in our apartment for a few hours before going back
to the gym for another (easier) workout of moderate strength and
stretching. The team would talk about how well we could do, what
teams to look out for, and who was strong and who was weak on
various events. We had really already prepared for competition,
so in these workouts, it was just a matter of maintaining shape
until we competed. Some athletes were more relaxed than others,

and some would vary in their emotions day to day or based on how training went for them on a particular day. Naturally it was intense, because we were at the Olympics and because we were very serious about competition. But at the same time, I think we all just enjoyed being there, and we tried to absorb it all.

The competition was held in sessions, and there was a drawing to determine which country would compete in which session. The earlier the session, the more of a disadvantage it was for those countries. This was because judges kept scores low in the morning. They knew they would see a lot of gymnastics throughout the day, and they needed room for the scores to go up for the other athletes later. In the Olympics or in any competition, in the last session, higher scores are much more common. If judges give somebody a perfect score in the early session, and someone comes in a later session with a better routine, there is no room to score that set higher. It's really unfortunate on all accounts. Steps have been taken to alleviate this problem, and a new scoring system is now in place that seems to be more just—sometimes.

Anyway, in Seoul, the scoring trend was very frustrating for the first session teams and a huge advantage for the last session teams. It was not right. And, unfortunately, the U.S. team drew to be in the first of three rotations, and this was really bad news for us. Everybody knew it was bad and that our scores would follow the trend, but there was nothing we could do about it. It grew even worse for us when we were told we had to compete first on three events. This was a freak thing that happened, because only four teams were in the first session as we started the competition. I think we all kind of thought we would not have a chance at a medal at this point, because there was seemingly no way to earn high enough scores, even if we hit our routines. Once we got through the shock of learning all of this, we kind of submitted to the fact that our job was to simply go out and do the best gymnastics we could do. That was all we could do. How we were judged was not up to us.

cɅɉɑ

Before we knew it, it was the first day of Olympic competition. The morning was just like any other morning, I guess. In theory, anyway. But, the day was different—of that, there was no question. I remember clearly that on that day, I started off by asking my roommate, Dominick, "What do you say? Do you want to compete in the Olympics today?"

I joked around a lot at the Olympics for two reasons. First, it is ingrained in my personality to be comical; it has always helped me to relax if I crack a joke or find a reason to smile. Secondly, it broke the tension that could have easily built up in the prolonged thought and silence of the "Olympic Morning." It worked, I think, because we both laughed as we headed to breakfast with the rest of the team.

After breakfast we were off to the gymnastics arena. Despite the attempts at jokes, I was nervous as we approached our venue. But, once I was actually in the arena, I felt much more relaxed. I had a fair amount of competition experience behind me, and although this was the Olympics, my body and mind slipped into a familiar routine—like an autopilot kind of thing—as had been the pattern in many other competitions. I warmed up, as I would have at any other meet.

It turns out that I was the first competitor in the 1988 Olympics, starting on vault. Incidentally, my mom was watching back in the States, and she told me later that she nearly fainted when the camera showed me first up. She went to the bathroom four times in the twenty minutes before I vaulted. Yeah, I was nervous, but my mom was REALLY nervous.

Back to vaulting. This first day of competition was the day of the easier routines: compulsories. I waited for my turn as patiently as I could. At the end of the runway by the judges, I could see a green light turn on. This meant that I had the go-ahead from the judges to perform my vault. I ran down, leaped over the horse, and turned one and a half times forward and landed with a small hop. It was a good start for me, and a good way for the U.S. to begin. But, my score was only 9.4. This was very low, and everybody knew it. It was then that our fears were confirmed: we were truly victims of the first session judging. Don't get me wrong; it wasn't like a "poor us," victim-mentality thing going on. It was just really unfortunate. Italy was in the first session with us, and their athletes had the same problem. All of us scored much lower than normal, and lower than expected, but we all knew there was nothing we could do about it. All we could do was give it our best and try to accept the results.

Each event passed and the U.S. did very well, with only a few mistakes here and there. I had a really good competition and no major breaks. When our first session was finished, we were in second place for our session, just slightly behind Italy. The rest of the countries competed throughout the day, and we looked on as the scoring got more generous. As the first day ended, the U.S. team was pushed to twelfth place. This was disappointing, but again, there was just nothing we could do about it. In all fairness, judging by the level of difficulty and the way we had competed, I feel we should have been somewhere around sixth at this time. But, that's just the way it was. We all have to learn to be good sports. We tried to focus on what went well, and really, despite our ranking, we did feel good about doing our job and competing well. But, I think all of us felt a bit defeated and helpless to move up. As for me, personally, I was happy with how I did on the first day and just concentrated on the fact that I would always compete against myself. I always wanted to beat my own scores. Quite honestly, that's a healthy way to view competition, and it helped to alleviate frustration if the scores of the other athletes surpassed my own.

So, day one ended. We had the "optionals" day ahead of us, and with optionals, we knew we could have a lot of room to move up in the rankings. The morning of the second day came fast. We had already reviewed and critiqued our first day of competition, and we were ready for the more difficult routines. After arriving at the arena, the day felt much like the first day. But, because these routines were more difficult than the compulsories, we warmed up for a little longer. Even so, the pattern of preparation was the same.

Competition began, and once more, we tried to perform to the best of our ability. After all, we had trained our whole lives for this moment. As a team, we competed well, but not great. Event by event, we were on a roller coaster of emotions. Our hopes increased as we watched our ranking improve some, but then our hopes were dashed as our ranking later fell back down. After all was said and done, the U.S. team finished in a disappointing eleventh place. In my opinion, if we had not been in that first compulsory session, we would have fared much better. Even so, the truth is that we just weren't strong enough at that point to be in medal contention as a team.

Despite the disappointing results of the team competition, I had a great meet and hit all six of my routines. I was very excited about how I did. If we finished high enough as individuals in the first round of competition, we would qualify for the individual all-around competition, which would decide the Olympic champion. After having a great meet on both days with no major mistakes, I did end up qualifying for the finals. I was eighteen years old and the second youngest competitor in the Olympics, just slightly older than one of the Soviet gymnasts. For me to qualify was a great surprise; no one had expected that from the "youngster." With the team competition behind me, I had to ready myself for the individual all-around finals. I felt as though I was an underdog, being so young, and this took a lot of the pressure off of me. There were still nerves, of course. There was just less pressure.

The day of the meet came. Unlike the team competition, I was alone out there. My teammates were there supporting me, of course, but it was an individual competition. I missed having that team feeling. My first event was high bar, one of my best events. I missed and fell on a release move. That was not the way I wanted to start. The first event was always the toughest to get through, though, so at least it was over with. I then went to floor exercise and had a hand touch down on my last pass. Once again, I made a careless mistake on a skill on which I was typically very consistent. Fortunately, for the rest of the competition, I did great. I finished the next four events without any noticeable or costly mistakes. Unfortunately, at that level, any mistake affects the ranking. And, even though medalling had been highly improbable anyway, I had made enough mistakes in my first two events to take me out of any medal contention. I knew I had had a rough start, but I got much better throughout the competition and I took comfort in that. But, I was disappointed that I had made major mistakes—any mistakes. Still, I was an Olympic finalist, and it was a great experience for me at such a young age.

The 1988 Olympic Games ended with the Soviet Union taking all but one gold medal out of all the individual events and the all-round. Sure, I was disappointed that things had not gone well for the U.S. team, but it was an incredible experience just to be there. Among other things, the first triple back flip to ever be performed on the floor exercise in an Olympics was done by Vladimir Gogoladze, a Soviet gymnast, right there in Seoul! Russian gymnast Valeri Liukin had successfully done one in a competition in Russia prior to the '88 Olympics, but for it to be done in an Olympics, right before the eyes of the world—well, it was incredible. I was really happy to witness a part of history up close. Honestly, I was thrilled to be a part of all that happened there, and I knew my experience would help me in the years to come.

We got to hang out with all the other athletes in the Olympic village for several days after our competition was over. It was cool and educational to talk with the Soviet gymnasts and other athletes from around the world about how they learned certain skills and trained in general. It was always a good idea to learn from the best. It was interesting to find out how different their training regimen was, and really how different their lives were from ours. But at the same time, it was fascinating to learn that they were very much like us. The sport, the dreams, the training—it brought us all together. Many of the Soviet gymnasts would become my good friends in the years to come. I had known about them from a distance before; in fact, they were intrigued that I knew so much about their careers, routines, and gymnastics. The sport was simply my passion, and if someone did good gymnastics, it just stayed with me.

I think a lot, and some say I analyze too much. But, thinking adds a lot to my life. Some of the thoughts I took away from the Olympics seemed to be pretty profound. They helped me in years to come. First, I learned that all we can do as gymnasts is our best, performing our routines and doing what we have trained to do. I knew I had tried to do that, and I had peace with that. At the Olympics or elsewhere, when I did my routines well, I always felt good, even if I did not win. The contrary was also true. Even if I won a competition, if I had not done my routines well, I felt bad. My job was to do as well as I could, and failure or success for me was decided not by judges or by rank but by doing what I set out to do. Don't get me wrong; winning is great, not only for the feeling, but also for the motivation to continue on. It drives athletes to reach for more. But apart from the winning or losing, success and failure—for me—are measured by whether or not my expectations for myself have been reached when I get to the end of a challenge. I believe that I did reach my personal expectations at the '88 Olympics. In fact, I may have even surpassed them, so for me, that experience was a success.

An interesting note: after making the Olympic team, I learned that sponsors would fly two members of my family to the Olympics to watch me compete. My mom has a fear of flying, so she didn't go. My dad and his father, my grandfather, jumped at the chance to go to the Olympics to watch me. They were very well taken care of while in Korea. All their expenses were covered, and they got to see other Olympic events as well as gymnastics. It was really exciting for me to have my dad and grandpa experience the Olympics just because I made the team.

As my dad and grandfather sat in the stands during the competition, Grandpa was looking all around him at the Korean and Japanese spectators. He said to my dad, "I can't believe this. Years ago in the war, we were killing each other. Now I'm sitting among them, enjoying this event and cheering for all the competitors."

When I heard about that exchange, I saw and understood the Olympics at yet another level. For my grandfather, after all he had experienced, seeing the world in a totally different way meant more to him than I would ever be able to comprehend. For him, it was a time of healing or relief, and for all of us, it was a time of profound unity of the world. For the two years following the Olympics, my grandfather would speak of the Olympics endlessly and always with joy and a smile on his face. Two years after the '88 Olympics, my grandfather passed away. The fact that my dad and grandfather got to be part of the Olympics together had special meaning to all three of us, and my grandfather's take on it opened my eyes to something I never expected.

Chapter 7

AFTER THE OLYMPICS

fter the 1988 Olympics, all of the United States Olympic athletes from all sports were invited to the White House to meet the President who, at the time, was Ronald Reagan. The total number of athletes representing the United States was around six hundred fifty. I traveled with the rest of the Olympic gymnastics team to Washington, D.C., for this honor. After passing through security and getting a small tour of the White House, all of the Olympic athletes met on the back lawn with the President to have lunch. It was a wonderful experience to be around such great athletes in so many different sports, and it was a humbling thing to be an invited guest of the President. Just being there was exciting—yet another experience I will never forget.

After getting back from the White House and having some light training and time off, the next thing on the agenda was the Olympic Gymnastics Tour. This was a tour featuring U.S. and Soviet gymnasts, and we went to about nine different cities in the United States, performing exhibitions in arenas for very large crowds. For me, this kind of thing is the most fun thing to do in gymnastics. On tour, I got to hang out with other gymnasts I admired and respected, and I was able to perform whatever routines I wanted in exhibition—free of judges—all while getting paid! All the athletes got along very well; it took us no time at all to realize that the atmosphere of a tour was much different from that of a competition. It was a time to be relaxed, to enjoy the sport, and to truly admire the skills of others. We did not have to be concerned about ranks and scores; we just had fun.

In 1989, I enrolled at the University of New Mexico. I chose not to take part in the NCAA program but to compete strictly for the United States, remaining on the National team. I was very limited at this time on how many college courses I could take, because I was competing internationally frequently. Still, I somehow managed to fit in several classes and earn several credits over the next few years in the midst of a very intense competitive schedule.

Because competition was intense, training was intense. And, it required learning different skills and combinations. After every Olympics, the rules and requirements for gymnastics change somewhat, so I had to change my routines, learn more skills, and adapt to those new rules. I made a lot of mistakes, but I was not alone in that. The first year of competition after the Olympics is always full of mistakes and experimenting. Everyone is trying to learn the new rules, and everyone is trying new skills. They really are not consistent as the experimenting begins, but that is the beauty of learning. Each year that passes before the next Olympics gets better for the athletes as they figure things out, train hard, and improve.

Skills weren't the only things that were new; faces were new. After the '88 Games, most of the Olympic team members retired. This meant that the U.S. needed new gymnasts so we could represent our country internationally and maintain our reputation as competitive in the world of gymnastics. I, as the youngest member on the '88 Olympic team, had a lot of good years ahead of me, so I did not retire. Because of that, I traveled all around the world to different meets, representing the U.S. in competitions as an Olympic gymnast. This was great on the one hand, as I gained a lot of experience and took part in many different competitions. But on the other hand, it was really hard work, and I was burning out a little. Some of the friends I had made were gone, so the atmosphere was different. Plus, I felt a little more pressure in the sport because people were viewing me as an Olympian, so there were always expectations. The judging was tough, the competition was tough, and the schedule was tough. The fans were great, though. I was actually surprised at how many fans of the sport recognized my accomplishments. Their support really carried me along.

Anyway, I did my best to maintain my training and competition regimen. After every competition, it was right back to the gym to prepare for the next meet, and I had no time to learn new skills in the gym. I missed that part of gymnastics, and again, because the rules had changed, I really needed that training time to work on new skills. In hindsight, I guess I should have declined a few competitions so I could relax a little bit, but my coach and I looked at every meet as an opportunity. But, an athlete has to maintain a balance. In this, I was way off.

I competed all summer long, and summer is normally the time a gymnast learns new skills. When the U.S. season began, I was already tired. I was in good shape, though, and I went to Winter Nationals with confidence. I had not changed my routines that much, but I had a great meet and won, becoming National Champion at age nineteen. I was really pleased with that accomplishment, but what I wanted more than anything else was to go into the gym and work new skills. I felt like I was starving for that. But, I couldn't take the time to satisfy that hunger. Working on new skills had to take a back seat to preparing for more competitions. Every competition was very important and had to be trained for properly. Thus, 1989 was the year I traveled the most and the year I experienced my first true burnout.

The build-up to burnout began in late 1989, when I went to China to compete in China's most prestigious competition: the China Cup. The traveling and the jet lag were very challenging.

Apparently, once or twice each year, a major windstorm blows from Mongolia into China. During my journey there, it happened. The storm set in, and our flight was diverted to Hong Kong where we would stay for the night and see if the weather would be good enough for us to get into Beijing the next morning. The report the next morning showed that the flight was still scheduled to go, so off we went. But, in mid-flight, we heard the announcement that the weather in Beijing was too bad for us to land. We were diverted again—this time to Shanghai. We stayed overnight and hoped for the next day to be better. We finally got to Beijing, but the two days we were supposed to have to adjust to jet lag and get used to the equipment had been used up in exhausting, frustrating travel. After landing in Beijing and spending only one night, the competition was one day away.

The best of the best were there to compete in the China Cup, and that was a huge motivation for me to do well. The first two events, vault and parallel bars, went really well for me, so I was off to a good start. I then went to high bar. As I was putting chalk on my hands getting ready to perform my routine, the grip I was wearing tore in half. A grip is a piece of leather that covers the hand and is secured around the wrist. It is used to prevent too many blisters, and it also offers tremendous help to the gymnast who, with it, can grip the bar more securely. Many grips feature a dowel, which allows for an even greater grip and more security. A torn grip is pretty bad news for a gymnast—a major equipment malfunction. I did not have a backup grip, so I asked my teammate if I could use one of his. He threw his grip to me. It takes a while to break grips in to fit a hand properly, and each gymnast has a little bit of a different fit. That is why gymnasts don't traditionally share their grips. This was a unique situation, though, and I figured that any grip would certainly be better than no grip at all.

I strapped the grip to my hand and continued to chalk up. I told the coach seconds before I mounted the bar that I could not do the Kovacs because of my grip, and he understood. A *Kovacs* is a release move where gymnasts do one and a half flips over the bar and then re-grab the bar. As I mounted the bar and did my first couple of skills, the grip felt different but not as different as I had expected, so I decided to perform the Kovacs anyway. As I launched myself flipping backwards and over the bar, I reached for the bar and wrapped my hands around it. I had it – or so I thought. At the bottom of my swing after catching my release move, my hands peeled off the bar and, with tremendous force, I was thrown flat on my back to the mat. It was a very hard landing, but my pride and spirit were hurt more than my body because I knew this fall would take me out of the top spots and likely out of medal contention.

When a gymnast falls off the event, he has thirty seconds to remount. I got up and put some more chalk on my hand, and I finished a very strong routine. The grip my teammate gave me as a quick replacement was just not fitted to my hand enough, so it did not allow me to grip the bar as efficiently as my own grip would have. When I think back on it, I realize I should never have attempted the Kovacs without my own grips, but with so little time to decide what to do, I was actually kind of proud that I went for it anyway. I just wish the result had been better—I ended up pretty low in the rankings. But, regardless of the rankings, I had a valuable experience.

As we were preparing to leave China, I received word that I had been invited to the White House for the "Great American Workout". This event was hosted by Arnold Schwartzenegger, who was the head of the U.S. Health and Fitness movement at the time. It was a very prestigious invitation, because only the Olympic athletes who were at the top of their sports were invited, and there were only about fifty of us. I flew from Beijing to San Francisco to Denver to Washington, D.C., and I arrived just in time for the breakfast that was hosted by Arnold Schwartzenegger. I had not had any good sleep for a very long time, and I had been in travel mode for almost thirty hours. Even so, it was a thrill to be there.

Like my previous visit to the White House, the event was held on the back lawn. Gymnastics equipment was set up on the grass and many TV celebrities, kids' athletic clubs and programs, and Olympians wandered the yard talking to the press, doing exhibitions and promoting the benefits of sports, fitness and health. The President (George H. W. Bush) and the First Lady walked about talking with everybody involved and thanking us for our participation. The event concluded with Arnold Schwartzenegger giving a speech about the direction he felt U.S. health and sport activity should go. It was a good event, and I was proud to be part of it.

After the speech, there was a reception, and we had the opportunity to socialize. It was a highlight for me to meet Arnold Schwartzenegger. After all, he was the star of The Terminator, along with a lot of those other great action movies. I thought that was cool. As I was leaving the White House grounds, I had a sneaking suspicion that it wouldn't be my last visit there. So, I looked at Arnold Schwartzenegger and said in a deep voice, "I'll be back." (Just kidding. I didn't really do that.)

My packed schedule continued, and though I used to be able to slack off before a small meet, this was not the case anymore as there were no small meets. Also, a lot of the travel continued to be overseas, and that can really wear on a person! It was a double-edged sword in that it was exciting to travel all over the world and compete in such great competitions, but it really took its toll on me. If I hadn't stayed alert, this dynamic could have drained me too much, and my performance could have suffered drastically. At first my coach was not all that concerned, but as the year rolled on, even he experienced burnout, and we both recognized it. We finally cancelled a couple of competitions, and it was at that point in my career that I learned how best to deal with burnout. As simple as it seems, I realized that in order to keep things fun and new, I had to make everything I did a game. I think people always learn faster when they are having fun. So, if I was training, I needed a challenge or a contest. I needed to play. This sounds easy but it is not. It is not supposed to be easy if you are already at the point of burning out. It was actually work to make it play—at first anyway.

Eventually, making training a game worked well for me, and it was fun. For example, my teammates and I would see who could do a new skill the best or get the closest to completing it. Finally, with this new approach, I got to play and learn new things in the gym. And, I got others involved, so I had a life again. I think they enjoyed it, too.

The 1989 season was busy, but toward the end of the season, I felt I had found my footing again. I qualified for my first World Championships to be held in Stuttgart, Germany. The World Championships is actually a much bigger competition than the Olympics for gymnastics as there are sixty countries represented there. The Olympics is much more prestigious, of course, with only the top twelve countries represented.

At Worlds, the rules were still new, and gymnasts from all around the world were trying new skills that they had not yet mastered. I was no different. Even with the new skills, I qualified for the all-around finals, just as I had at the Olympics. There were only two sessions (that was better than three), but unfortunately, I was in the first of those two sessions. I had a great competition and was in first place in the first all-around session until I reached my last event—imagine deadly and dramatic music here—the pommel horse. This event was still my nemesis. It never changed. Just as was the case years before, I was great on horse in training. But in competition, I had trouble controlling my nerves. It just seemed like something I could not master. So, there in Germany, I jumped up and started swinging around the horse and traveling backwards across it. About halfway through my travel, my hand slipped and I was off. Just like that. I did manage to finish the routine pretty well, but the damage was done. As I stayed and watched the second session of athletes, I could see the scores were higher and my rank was being pushed further downward. I couldn't complain; I was responsible because I had fallen. My rank kept dropping, and I ended up in twenty-fourth place. I probably would have been around tenth without the fall. Saying "would have been" and "could have been" doesn't change the end result, but it can help an athlete to see where he could be if he could fix his mistakes.

Competing at Worlds was a great experience for me and once again, I learned a lot from watching gymnasts from the other fifty-nine countries compete. It also solved my burnout problem; I went back to the U.S. more motivated than I had been for years. I knew that if I could just fix a few things, I could be much closer to the top. Also, I was still working on some new skills, and I knew that once I mastered them, I could definitely improve my ranking. With the burnout extinguished, it was time for the re-growth. I was ready, and I was excited.

Chapter 8

GOODWILL GAMES

After the 1989 World Championships, the next step for me was to try to qualify to compete in the Goodwill Games. The Goodwill Games are held every four years, and they include more countries than the Olympics. The Goodwill Games stand as one of the three world ranking competitions in the world, along with the Olympics and World Championships. However, only four gymnasts from each country can qualify to go to the competition. In the United States, we only had one national competition that was used as the qualifier for the Goodwill Games. It was held in Minnesota in July of 1989. I went into the meet with a lot of confidence, and I had a great competition with the exception of parallel bars. It was on p-bars that I gave the national title away by letting my feet hit the ground as I swung through the bottom of the bars. That was a huge disappointment, and it was beginning to seem as though I would always have a mistake somewhere to hold me back from a great finish. I always walked away wondering how high I could really finish if I didn't have any mistakes. Though I was frustrated in Minnesota, it didn't bother me too much because I ended up in third place, so I qualified for the Goodwill Games. That had been my goal, and I was on my way.

The training camp for the Goodwill Games was held at Gold Cup in Albuquerque, my home gym. It was a tremendous advantage to be able to train where I was comfortable and familiar. The other three athletes on the team were John Roethlisberger from Minnesota, who went on to make three Olympic teams during his career, Chris Waller from California, who became a member of the

1992 Olympic team, and Trent Dimas, my teammate at Gold Cup. It was a very strong team. I was in the best shape of my life, and I was very excited to try to put it all together and have a great meet, and to see where I placed in the world.

The Goodwill Games were to be held in Tacoma, Washington, another great advantage for our country. The Goodwill Games were very much like the Olympics, as there were all the different sports represented and athletes who all stayed in the Goodwill Games Village. Just as it had been for the Olympic Trials and the Olympics, media was out of control. After all, it was a huge competition, and it was being held in our country. Four years before, the very first Goodwill Games had been in Russia, and they were created there to be a demonstration of the "good will" shared between the Soviet Union and the United States, with invitations to the rest of the world to join in. It was an extremely prestigious event; the Soviet Union regarded it as second only to the Olympics. This time, it was on home turf, which allowed the United States to continue the advances toward good will. The U.S. team was ready and strong, and the whole world seemed to be excited about the meet.

After a couple of days getting settled into our dorm rooms and exploring the village, we began our training in the large arena. We used our first training session to get used to the new equipment. Training was going very well until I reached vault. During my vaulting workout I rolled my ankle a little on a landing, but I did not think too much of it at the time. As I continued to train on the other events, however, it grew worse. It became a point of concern, and when I began my floor training it was much too sore to do my routine. We concluded training that day and went back to the dorm. I was depressed about my ankle, but the plan was to see how it was for the next day of training. I iced it and did all that I could to rest up and prepare for the next day's training. When I woke up, it was very sore, but I figured that once I got it warmed up a little it would feel better. We arrived at the arena for our second day of training, and as I began to warm up, I grew very concerned. My ankle was tight, and I still could not do my floor routine. My coach and I decided to make some changes to my set. I replaced my normal mount (a double layout flip) with a laid out one-and-a-half-twisting one-and-three-quarter-flip to a rollout. This was still a very difficult skill and equal in difficulty to the double layout. But, because I could roll out of this replacement skill, we felt it would be easier for my ankle. I was disappointed to have to make the change, but I was relieved to find a viable solution. The rest of training went well for me, so I ended the day feeling pretty good.

We arrived back at our dorm and settled in to get as much rest as we could. There was a lot of pressure surrounding this event, and being in the U.S., I felt it more than usual. I just wanted so badly to do well and to be at my best.

It was always difficult for me to sleep the night before a major competition. I would juggle or play chess with my teammates to stop obsessing about the following day. This did help a lot, and eventually, I could sleep. Not that night, though. I was still pretty concerned about my ankle. I had come to the meet in the best shape of my life, and then I had to go and hurt my ankle. It really bothered me, and I really struggled with my thoughts over the whole thing before finally falling asleep. Morning came, and I woke up with the familiar feeling of "this is the day of competition." I think I must have gotten a lot of my stress out the night before by just thinking things to death because I felt fairly relaxed. The team went to breakfast and then on to the arena.

As we entered the building, cheers swelled. After all, we were the home team! It was amazing to hear the crowd calling out for us, and we did not want to disappoint them. I have to say that once I arrived at the meet sight and heard the cheering, I kind of went straight into competitive mode. I think this came from having so much competitive experience by this point. My mind and body relaxed, and my system seemed to go through the same process it had gone through at any other competition I took part in. I did not worry about my ankle or my routines. I just naturally focused. I loved the fact that my mind and body had become this way. It made me a much better competitor over the years, and I do think this is something that only comes with experience.

We started to warm up and I felt pretty good. I felt my ankle throb a little, but it was wrapped very tightly and was not bothering me much at all. I was pleased that I felt so little pain. This was the team competition, and if I did well enough there, I would qualify for the all-around finals as I had done in the Olympics and Worlds. I was hoping for that, but I knew I needed to focus on the team competition first.

The U.S. did very well, with very few mistakes. My mistakes came on my modified floor routine and my ring landing. Both mistakes were probably due to my weakened ankle, but the rest of my events were above average and I felt good about the competition. Not great, but good, and I knew I could do better if I qualified for the all-around competition. Even pommel horse, my nemesis, went very well, and I was excited about that. The U.S. did great and finished with a silver medal, right behind the Soviet Union. That was a major accomplishment for us, especially after the Soviets had run away with everything in the '88 Olympics. After that, it seemed as if we couldn't touch them. But, there we stood, next to them on the podium, and we all felt really great about it. The media was everywhere, and we were more than happy to share our feelings with them. The event was heavily televised, and it felt good to know that the rest of the country could see what we had done.

Within a half-hour after the competition, the names of the competitors who qualified for the all-around finals were released. Only two gymnasts per country were allowed to qualify for the AA finals. I ended up finishing second on the U.S. team, with scores high enough to qualify. I was really happy because with my two mistakes, I knew it would be close. I also knew I could do better, and I really wanted the chance to prove it.

We had one day off while the girls had their meet. That gave my weak ankle more time to rest and heal. After winning the silver in the team competition, I was more relaxed, and I felt I could really go all out in the all-around. Besides, I had a silver medal already, and that took some pressure off of me.

The all-around finals came quickly, and the day began just as the team competition did: breakfast and then straight to the arena. My ankle felt much better in warm up than it had two days before, and I felt surprisingly relaxed. I think because I had already had a full competition with the team event, I was much more at home on the equipment and in the arena in general. My first event was pommel horse. I knew if I could hit my routine on horse, the most challenging part of my meet would be over. After all, once I had faced the nemesis, I had all my best events to come. Controlling my nerves, I hit one of the best pommel horse sets I have ever done. It was the kind of start to competition a gymnast dreams about. The next event was rings. I had had trouble in the team competition on my dismount, but not this time. I completed a very strong routine with no problem on the landing. Next was vault. I had a small hop on the landing, but it was very solid. Next up: p-bars. I would be doing my new front one-and-three-fourths flip between the bars, and if that went well, it would help my score a lot. I ended up doing one of the best routines on parallel bars; my new trick went perfectly, and I finished well, sticking the landing cold. After each event, I could see my ranking posted on the Jumbotron (electronically posted scores), and I knew I was steadily moving up. I was in fifth place going into my last two events. That meant I was in medal contention for the world all-around title. It was pretty intense.

High bar was next. Although high bar was my best event, I was going to be performing that very difficult new release move, the Kovacs. My routine also had a very difficult dismount—a double layout with two twists. There was a lot of risk in play, but I was ready to roll. I mounted the bar just as I had in training. I threw the Kovacs, and it worked out to be just the right length from the bar for me to catch it smoothly. I followed that with two more risky release moves, in combination. Just the dismount remained. I swung around the bar in preparation, and then I hurled my body through the air with two flips and two twists in the laid out position, and I landed with only a small hop. I rocked my high bar routine! This launched me into third place. If I could just hit my floor routine, I would be able to walk away from the Goodwill Games with a bronze medal for the all-around. That was huge! I concentrated on staying calm, but I knew what was at stake with this last routine. My ankle was no longer a factor to me in my mind, so I just concentrated on doing each tumbling pass the best that I could. I began with no problem or pain on my first pass. The second pass—the one I had had trouble with in the team competition—also went perfectly. Third pass, no problem. Standing in the corner before my last pass, I knew this was it. If I landed okay, I would be third in the world with a bronze medal, and if I missed I would receive nothing. No pressure there, right? After springing up and flipping two times in the air, I landed with just a small hop and clinched my fists as I knew I had just achieved the rank of third best gymnast in the world all-around, earning a bronze medal! The first two spots went to Soviet gymnasts, which made my medal even more special to me. I stood up there on the podium with gymnasts who had blown everyone away in the Olympics. Now, I was with them. I was one of them. I can't express the feeling; it was incredible.

Winning that bronze medal was the highlight of my gymnastics career up to that point. After all the years of training and wanting to show what I was capable of doing, I finally had a meet where it all came together for me. Calling it "fulfillment" doesn't seem to do it justice. This was what I had been working for all my life. That entire night I was just so excited and felt so good that I never wanted it to end. The other athletes from other sports I would run into in the village had all seen it on TV, and they were congratulating me. The two Russian gymnasts who placed first and second also congratulated me, and that meant a lot. Most importantly, though, I had come to the Goodwill Games ready to do what I had trained to do, and under so much pressure and with a minor injury, I had succeeded. I had reached my goal.

One might think that victory brought the Goodwill Games to an end. That is not the case; the competition was not over for me. In the team preliminaries, I had qualified to compete for an individual medal on the vault, on parallel bars, and on high bar. I was scheduled to compete in the individual events two days after I took the bronze in the all-around. I was very relaxed, and I was ready to go all out on the individual events. I felt I had nothing to lose, as this competition had already been a huge success for me. So, it was time to give it my all.

My first event in the event finals was vault. In finals, gymnasts have to do two different vaults. I had one strong vault and one average vault. I did my best vault first, and I stuck the landing cold. On my second vault, I took a small step, but the difficulty was not very high so I scored much lower. Because I was first up on the vault, I had to wait for the other athletes to complete their vaults to see if I had a chance for a medal. One by one, I saw my rank fall until I was out of the medal hunt. I was a little disappointed, but I was still so ecstatic about the all-around and pumped for the other events that I just moved on.

My next event was parallel bars. I had the third highest score going into the finals. My performance was a duplicate of my performance in the all-around competition except for a small hop on the landing. Still, it was good enough to earn a bronze medal—my third medal of the competition. I was very happy, naturally, but my mind quickly turned to my next and final event, high bar. I was last up in the competition on high bar, and that was an advantage. I could see what scores and routines I had to beat to get a medal. Trent Dimas, my teammate from the U.S., had been one of the favorites, but he fell from the bar and that took him out of medal contention. Both Soviet gymnasts did very well, and the all-around world champion, Vitali Scherbo, scored a nearly perfect 9.9. After seeing that, I felt I could possibly get a silver or a bronze, but my focus was still on just successfully competing my set. Doing what I was trained to do.

It was intense. The pressure was on. The time had come.

A funny story: this competition was being aired live in the U.S., and just as I was about to mount the high bar, the network took a commercial break. Later I learned that Mom and Dad and all my friends at home who were watching went absolutely nuts, because they knew it was live and because they couldn't see how I was doing. They thought they were missing it all, and they knew it was all happening just on the other side of that commercial. Anyway, all was well, because when they came back from the break, they heard the commentator say, "From just moments ago, here is Lance Ringnald on high bar." They proceeded to show my high bar routine, commenting on every skill. Each successful release combination drew cheers from the crowd and brought out great comments from the announcers. As I landed with a small hop, I knew that I had won another medal. I just did not know what color. When the judges finished their conference, the score was posted. It was 9.9! I tied with the best gymnast in the world for a gold medal on high bar! To be the best in the world on any event in gymnastics is a dream come true. To win gold for the U.S. while competing in front of a U.S. crowd is indescribable. That moment, along with becoming an Olympic gymnast, still lives with me today as my proudest moment as a gymnast.

Chapter 9

OVERCOMING INJURY

Following my once-in-a-lifetime experience at the Goodwill Games, I returned to my gym in Albuquerque to resume my "regular" life. Workouts were light at first, but they became more demanding as I spent a lot of time working new skills and perfecting old ones. As I have mentioned, gymnastics is a seasonal sport when it comes to competition, but training goes on all year long. If I ever took too much time off, it would have been very hard to get back into shape again. I never wanted to have to do that, so time off was not really an option.

So, going with that subject of being "in shape," let me explain some things. My body fat percentage for the Goodwill Games was between two point five and four percent. Gymnasts use large muscle groups in a much wider range of motion than athletes in other sports do. Before a major competition, training could last as long as six hours each day, including not only practice of the routines, but also a LOT of strength and stretching programs. With so much time lifting, swinging, bouncing, and pressing the human body around, my low body fat percentage was not unusual; it was a common thing for gymnasts to have such low body fat. Gymnasts are known for their strength, flexibility, and acrobatic agility. I believe that pound for pound, gymnasts are the strongest athletes in the world. Generally, gymnasts are small, and being small is actually beneficial. The smaller a person is, the easier it is to have a higher strength to weight ratio. Think of an ant. Studies show that one ant can easily lift around ten other ants over its head. Laws of physics say the smaller the body mass, the less gravity there is to act against it. That same principle works for gymnasts, especially on events such as rings and floor exercise. Now, when it comes to high bar and parallel bars, it is actually beneficial to be a little taller and a little bit slender, because speed and lines are so important. Besides, it looks great when gymnasts built that way can maintain their lines in competition. It's very aesthetically pleasing! Their lines add something special, and often, it is not what skills gymnasts are doing but how well, how uniquely, and how beautifully gymnasts do those skills that counts. Anyway, to define what the perfect body is for gymnastics is difficult because the different events demand different physical characteristics. Flexibility is vital for a gymnast, no matter what the build. Being flexible makes certain skills possible, and it makes all the skills that a gymnast executes look much better. Also, when bending the body in all sorts of different positions, flexibility helps to prevent injury. Injury prevention is very important for the longevity of athletes.

Okay, enough of that. Back to competition. After the Goodwill Games, the next major competition in my sights was the World Championships of 1991, to be held in Indianapolis, Indiana. Once again, a worldwide competition was to be held on American soil— our home turf—so it promised to be a great opportunity. With the recent success of the Goodwill Games and going into the Worlds ranked third in the world as well as first on high bar, this was a great political advantage for me and for the U.S. team in general.

To get to that competition, I first had to qualify for the World team. Along with the Goodwill Games, I had had many successful competitions in 1990, and I won the U.S. vs. Romania all-around title in 1991. However, National Championships, to be held in Cincinnati, Ohio, would be used as the qualifier for the Worlds, so doing well there had to be my goal. I knew I would have to focus on that rather than on my previous accomplishments. So, I was off to Cincinnati. I was in very good shape going into Nationals, and expectations were that I would do very well. But, the scoring system was going to be different, so I could not let my guard down for a minute. Normally, final scores were based on a combined score, with 50% from compulsories and 50% from optional competition. The USGF changed the rules only for the 1991 Nationals to emphasize the quality of the compulsory routines, knowing ahead of time that the session we would compete in the second day at Worlds would be decided by how well we did in the compulsories. If we did well, we would compete in a later session the next day, and that would be to our benefit. To help with our mindset and the judges' consideration, the National scores were tallied as 60% compulsories and 40% optionals. It would go back to the regular 50/50 at Worlds.

I had a very good first day in the National compulsories until my "nemesis," the pommel horse, bit me hard. After banging my leg on the horse and almost coming to a stop, I had to muscle myself back into the rhythm of a routine, and that cost me dearly. Compulsories are judged much more strictly than optionals are because they are more basic. I finished in a disappointing seventh place after the compulsories. This was going to make it much more difficult to become national champion and even to qualify for the World Championships. This was not the way I wanted to start. My coach and I knew that my optionals were much stronger than my compulsories, but we also knew I would have to have an exceptionally good day on optionals to make up for my mistakes.

While warming up for the optional competition, I felt the pressure to qualify for Worlds pretty intensely, but I still warmed up very well. Optionals went great for me, and even my pommel horse score was above normal. I won the optionals very decisively. Under the normal 50/50 rules, I would have won the National Championships. Unfortunately, however, with the 60/40 alteration for this competition, I finished in fifth place. That was pretty disappointing. But, because of my comeback in optionals, I was able to qualify for the World Championship team, so I met one of my goals. And, deep inside, and considering the normal rules for the World Championships, I knew I was going into the Worlds ranked first in the U.S. That was a great feeling. I was pretty confident going in, but I knew that I could not make the same mistake at Worlds that I had made at Nationals.

Anytime a major competition was held in our country, it was a strange advantage—a good one, but a strange one. There was always much more pressure and press surrounding the event. This was exactly the scene at Worlds in 1991. Cameras and microphones were everywhere, and the heat was on. It was an exciting place to be—for the press and for us.

The team met in Indianapolis about two weeks before Worlds for a training camp. Everybody was in very good shape, and as we were all really close friends, we had a lot of team camaraderie. The training camp went very well for the entire team. About one week before Worlds started, we had a practice competition. Once again, I felt like I was in the best shape of my life, and I won this competition. I did have a small problem when I did the one-and-three-quarter front flip between the parallel bars, but I pulled it out. This was the same skill that helped me win bronze in the Goodwill Games the year before. It's a skill that is very hard on the body, and it puts a great deal of pressure on the arms when it is landed. I completed it successfully, but something wasn't right. I hurt what I thought was my shoulder, at the time. It was not that painful, but I knew something had happened that was not natural for me. I did not think much of it for the rest of the day, and after awhile, my shoulder felt almost normal. However, in the following day of training, I noticed some weakness in my shoulder. I could still do all my skills, but my shoulder felt funny. It was a small pain, but the weakness was noticeable. Because it was only one week before Worlds, I could not lay off training at all. But, as training continued, I felt my shoulder getting more and more sore. I told the coaches about it, so we changed workouts as much as we could to go easy on the shoulder. That did help a little, but I felt as if it was still getting worse. It was hurting more and more each day.

After a few days, my shoulder was extremely sore, but I was still getting through my routines very well. There were only two skills that really brought out the pain. The first was a jam on the high bar, which included scooping my legs through my hands and then shooting my feet out while dislocating my shoulders ("dislocating" is a gymnastics term, by the way; they weren't literally dislocated), then hanging onto the bar with my hands turned around one hundred eighty degrees. Nothing to it, right? Right. I could still do the skill, but it hurt quite a bit. The other skill that caused me a lot of pain was the iron cross on rings. The iron cross was normally very easy for me. With my shoulder being hurt, however, it was very painful. With only two days remaining before the competition, my coach and I had to decide if I should try to compete or if we should let the alternate compete. John Roethlisberger was the alternate, and he was very ready and able to compete if I could not. It was a hard decision, because I was definitely hurting. But, based on what I had been able to do in training, we finally decided that I would compete. This was very stressful for me, but obviously I had to do the best I could do. I wanted to do well, of course, and I had to consider what was best for the team. I was recognized internationally at this point, and to not compete might lower the team score. After all, only two skills were affected by my sore shoulder. The rest of my routines were still very solid.

In the first day of compulsory competition, I started on floor. I hit a very strong routine, so I was off to a good start. My next event was the pommel horse. Unlike the fiasco at Nationals, my routine was very strong. I felt very relieved to have this event behind me, and I was even more relieved to have a very good score.

My concern quickly turned to my shoulder, because rings was my next event. Rings was one of my best events normally, but with the shoulder problem, I knew it was going to hurt. I began my rings routine very strong—"business as usual." As I lowered into the iron cross, I had no problem. Just like on pommels, I was relieved. After holding the cross with minimal pain, I proceeded to transition into the next skill. Then, everything changed. As I lowered back to hang upside down, I felt a very unnatural movement in my shoulder. This feeling was accompanied by a sound like that of tearing Velcro—a sound I was told later that even the surrounding judges could hear. It wasn't exactly painful; it just felt incredibly unnatural. That is the only way I know to describe it. I remember an intense burning sensation, and I remember the sound. As I hung upside down on the rings in the middle of World Championships with my shoulder throbbing and on fire, I did not know what to think. I attempted the next trick in my routine, and my arm refused to work. I did a small swing, but as I pulled down on the rings to swing to a handstand, there was no pressure to help me launch into the handstand. With no other options, I casually did a small basic flip off the rings and landed on my feet. Aside from feeling the heat in my shoulder, my only thought was, "I hope I am hurt enough to have just legitimately jumped off the rings in the middle of World Championships."

It is odd what one thinks about in extraordinary times.

As I said, I was kind of casual about the whole thing. I jumped down, I was vaguely aware of a possibly very confused arena full of spectators, and I slowly turned around and walked toward my coach while softly rubbing my shoulder. The trainer approached me and asked what happened. I was not in that much pain, but I knew my arm was hurt badly. I told the trainer what I could about what had happened. I was quickly taken back into the training room where several different trainers looked me over and made various predictions of what had likely happened. The conclusion at the time was that nobody could truly know what I had done until I had an MRI. This would allow the doctors to see what had happened to any tissue in my arm. With that, my competition was over, and the men's team would have to compete with a missing team member. It was hard to accept that, for the team and for me, but really, I was more concerned with my arm at the time.

I had an MRI the following day, and though it was still not clear, the problem appeared to be a torn pectoralis major tendon. I returned to the competition—as a spectator, this time—with my arm in a sling. I watched the rest of the World Championships from the sidelines, cheering on my team as they went on to finish in fifth place. Not bad for having an absent team member! It was really hard to watch them compete without me, and it brought out a lot of emotions in me. Yet, I had to face the hard facts: there was nothing I could do about it. I did my best to support my team, and they were all very supportive and encouraging to me. It was strange, being injured. I had known that I was going to feel a lot of pain in the competition, but I never thought my body would actually break. I thought that the pain I had been feeling just fell into the usual sore muscle category of pain, but I was wrong. I learned then that as an athlete, it is important to listen carefully to the body and to take good care of it. We need to do all we can to prevent and/or avoid future injury. It was a hard, valuable lesson.

I returned to Albuquerque, but shortly after that, I flew to Vail, Colorado, where I met Dr. Richard Hawkins. Dr. Hawkins was a surgeon and a shoulder specialist, and the USGF recommended him due to his expertise in his field. He decided that the first thing I had to do was to get a better MRI, as the one taken in Indianapolis was not very clear. My second MRI was much clearer, and it showed exactly what had happened. Dr. Hawkins and I then talked about my options. Basically, he explained that if I did not have surgery, I would lose up to seventy percent of the strength in my arm. That was not an option, of course, so we decided to schedule surgery. Dr. Hawkins was aware of my status as an Olympic athlete, and he had helped many other Olympic and professional athletes, so I had a lot of respect for him. I trusted that he would fix me up right.

Surgery was scheduled for the next day. During the operation, when they got to my pectoralis major, they found that the tendon had completely torn away from the humerus (the upper arm bone). Thus, that ripping Velcro sound. During the two hours of surgery, they had to drill eight holes in my humerus and reattach the torn tendon with heavy gauged wire to holes in the bone. The wire was one that would remain there permanently. It was pretty intense surgery. Just a side note: as a world-class gymnast, I had very little fat on me, so there was very little to obstruct the view of what the doctors were doing. So, they filmed the surgery in order to use it as a teaching video. This flattered me. I watched that video after it was completed, and I was truly amazed at what Dr. Hawkins accomplished.

I was in the hospital in Colorado for one day before we drove from Vail back to Albuquerque. Before, during, and after surgery, I had very little pain. What I hated the most was being so nauseated after the operation. In a matter of hours though, that passed. For the next four weeks, I was in a sling and could not move my arm much at all.

My sling was removed a month after surgery, and then it was time for rehab. I met with the therapist, and we talked about how best to proceed. Everyday, I started with basic, light stretches for my shoulder. Then, basically, I spent a couple of hours doing simple range of motion and low load weight exercises until it became easier for me. I had trained very hard all my life, so this stuff was pretty easy for me and my shoulder never really felt that much pain.

About six weeks after surgery I kicked up to my first handstand on the floor. My shoulder was very tight and very weak. It was not accustomed to being used. As my shoulder got better from continuous rehab, I went into the gym and started going through some basic skills. I was surprised at how fast my body wanted to get back to its previous shape. There was some serious muscle memory, I guess, and my muscles really craved being where they had been before. I noticed pretty quickly that my shoulder worked a bit differently than before. The tendon was attached just a little lower than it had been previous to the injury, and this made the tendon much tighter. My surgeon said that once I had stretched it out more, it would feel normal and even stronger because it was attached lower. Over time I found that to be true.

Healing and rehab were really intense for me because my ultimate goal was to try to qualify for the 1992 Olympic Games. Working toward that goal was one of the biggest challenges I had ever faced. I had very little time, and I did not know how long everything would take to heal, so my future was unclear. That was difficult for me. I had no other choice, though, than to just accept my situation. I decided that I would just do the best that I could do, and what would happen would happen. It was all in God's hands. That became a very strong philosophy of mine, and it lasted throughout the remainder of my career. I decided to do everything I could to achieve what I set out to achieve, and if I didn't reach my goals, I would at least always have peace knowing that I did all I could do. If I did not do everything possible to achieve my goals, then I knew I would be stuck with the "what if I had done more" thought, and this would never have set well with me. That's a philosophy I still hold on to today—that, and the knowledge that everything is in God's hands.

Chapter 10

GETTING THROUGH THE TRIALS

My injury happened in September of 1991, and by January of '92, four months after my surgery, I was back to doing about sixty percent of my gymnastics skills. The first competition I would have to take part in to qualify for the 1992 Olympic team was the National Championships to be held in May. This gave me about four months to prepare. It was going to be very close. Not only did I have to get my skill level back, but I also had to be in peak competition form. As I trained, I noticed that some positions hurt my arm a lot, so I had to stay away from skills that put me in those positions. My coach and I decided to take out the front one and three quarter flip I had done in my parallel bar routine since that was most likely the cause of the initial tearing of my tendon at Worlds. Rings also had to be changed, so my coach and I had to create new routines for both p-bars and rings.

I continued rehab, and I grew stronger as time went on. Three weeks before Nationals, I was doing ninety percent of my sets, but they had been modified a little and did not have the difficulty that they had before. I did not like that, but I recognized it as being necessary to avoid both the pain and the possibility of re-injuring my shoulder. It was around this time that I attempted to hold the iron cross by myself again. I had been doing a lot of strength to prepare my shoulder for this skill, but I was nervous when actually attempting it. My surgeon assured me that it was okay to put the full force of the cross onto my shoulder, though, so one day I jumped up on rings and without too much thought, slowly lowered into a cross. It felt a little tight, but I actually held it for an easy five seconds. This was a great confidence booster, and although I was not doing my most difficult routines, I knew I would be ready for Nationals.

By the time we left for Nationals, I felt that I was still only about ninety percent physically, but I was pretty comfortable with my routines. I did not know how to feel going into the meet, and I really had no idea how I would do against the rest of the gymnasts as I had not seen them for six months and was not sure what kind of shape they were in. Of course at Nationals, everyone is usually in good shape, especially in an Olympic year. Throughout the year as gymnasts see each other at meets, they are able to gauge who has momentum and who does not. I was not too worried about my shoulder, but I really had no idea how I would stack up against the other athletes. Once again, I took comfort in the fact that I felt I had done everything possible to get my body and mind ready for this event, and I was there to do the best I could with what I had. I intended to give it my all so I could leave with no regrets.

It was good to see all my gymnastics friends again. The media seemed more intense than usual to me at this Nationals because they had many questions about my rehab and how I felt about my gymnastics since the injury. Because I was so established and had many accomplishments behind me, it was the U.S. Gymnastics Federation's hope that I could get back to being on the Olympic team. Of course I wanted this also, but for it to happen, I needed to hit in competition.

I started the first day of the meet as I had started many meets before. On rings, halfway through my set, I lowered into the iron cross and held it for three seconds with no problem. Because of my shoulder, I had to bend my arms in order to get out of the iron cross. Though there was a small deduction for that, it was necessary to avoid too much stress on the shoulder. I had a great first day and finished in sixth place. That felt great, and it gave me a much needed boost of confidence. Of course after the first day, I was only halfway done. But, after so much time away from competition and not knowing how I might do at Nationals, I already felt as though I had made a successful comeback just by being there and by making it through the day.

Many people had not believed I would get back to being healthy and strong enough to compete at Nationals. Their attitude wasn't one of cruelty; they simply knew the shoulder injury I suffered was a major one, and they knew making it back would be really difficult. Gymnastics is not the kind of sport where anything less than one hundred percent is healthy enough to be competitive at such a high level. As I was recovering, everyone had looked to me to give them answers regarding my plans for the future, my thoughts about competition, and what my health would be. But in truth, there was just no way of knowing. I could never have told them what the future held. In the same way, I would have never been able to tell anyone that when I mounted rings at Worlds that day that my chest muscle was going to tear away. Life is full of uncertainties. But, as it does with many other athletes, knowing that some people doubted me and my ability fed the fire inside, motivating me even more to show them that they were wrong and that I would come back. That "doubt" thing is an interesting and powerful motivational tool. Making a comeback was the biggest challenge of my life, especially because I was very limited on time to get back to normal health. All of that combined made doing so well on that first day of Nationals even more satisfying.

Media coverage remained intense at the meet. It was even more intense for me after the first day of competition. I remember saying redundantly that I felt great about finishing so well after the first day and getting back to the point where I was, but that I still had a second day of competition and that I did not want to think too much about things until I had completed the entire competition. My statements, though repetitive, were absolutely true. Though I was satisfied with my first day, I did still need to focus on that second day. Optionals would be more challenging for me anyway, so that's where my mind needed to be.

On the second day of competition, I warmed up well and felt pretty relaxed. I completed a very good pommel horse routine, which was my biggest relief. But, I still had to compete on rings. The rings routine went very well, and although it was a less difficult routine than the one I was competing before my injury, I still scored well with a solidly hit routine.

After all six routines were completed, I truly felt like I had succeeded in my comeback. I finished sixth in the all-around, and I qualified for the Olympic Trials to be held in Baltimore about three weeks later. I felt great, and I was much more relaxed after making it through the meet. Everyone was happy; the media seemed happy to report a "feel good story," and I was happy to be heading to Trials. Normally, I would have wanted to be ranked higher going into Trials, but after all that I had gone through in the previous six months, I was thrilled just to make it through the competition. I hadn't been able to compete for all that time, so being sixth at Nationals felt incredible. I was in Olympic team contention, and it was what I needed after Nationals.

The day after Nationals, we traveled back home to Albuquerque to start getting ready for Trials. Once again, only the top eighteen gymnasts in the country qualified for Trials, and everybody was in great shape. It was my second time around, so I had experience on my side. That helped me deal with all I needed to go through to prepare. And actually, we did not change training that much. The way I trained before Nationals had really worked for me, and if it was working, we did not want to change it. I do believe I got stronger and healthier in the three weeks before the Trials, but the time surely passed quickly. Before we knew it, we were off to Baltimore.

Being at the Olympic Trials was different for me this time, because I was a veteran in the world of gymnastics. When I was eighteen, I had no idea what to think about anything, so I just went about my competition without a care in the world. This time, I knew what it felt like to make an Olympic team, and I wanted nothing more than to feel those feelings again. Also different for me was that I was aware I was not capable of doing my best gymnastics due to the injury, and that would make qualifying for the team very challenging. I had many mixed emotions as I entered the Trials. On the one hand, I was very happy to have dealt with my injury and to have worked at rehab intensely enough that I could get back to the point of being almost where I had been before the injury. That gave me a deep sense of accomplishment. On the other hand, my shoulder was still a thorn in my side, and it was very stressful entering Trials not being one hundred percent (or at least the one hundred percent I wanted).

As is normal with the Olympic Trials, media coverage was intense, and there were always several questions about the state of my shoulder. I ran out of things to tell the reporters. My words just became repetitive. Here I was at the Trials. I qualified for the Trials in sixth place. Only time would tell how things would work out. As a competitor, I tried not to over-think things too much.

Regarding that "thinking" thing . . . it may be a strange thing to mention, but sometimes the mind can get in the way. Many people might identify with the behavior of the mind when it is under pressure. When I was in the 1988 Olympics and competing on the pommel horse, I remember that during my performance, I was actually thinking about what the team was going to do later that night. I wondered, "Are we going to play cards in our dorm, or maybe watch a movie?" This happened occasionally to me in different competitions during my career. It has occurred to me since then that sometimes, when under pressure, the mind will wander and think the craziest thoughts. It's just a break in concentration, maybe a defense from the nerves or something, and even though it was not intentional during meets, for me it would just happen sometimes. That is why I trained so hard and did my routines over and over. I hoped that if my mind began to wander and lose its focus, my body would be so programmed that the muscle memory would take over and continue with the routine I had trained my body to do (a very literal definition of the word "routine"). I noticed that many times after I completed a set, I could not recall the specific details of the routine. The different elements or the dismount would seem like a blur. But then, at other times, it would feel like I was competing in slow motion and I could recall every movement and every detail of every skill I performed. In some competitions, I would be more nervous than in others, and sometimes I would be more focused than at other times. To this day, I am not sure what would cause me to feel differently in meets. I just learned that no matter how I felt, preparing properly for a competition was the best way to ensure success. There were no shortcuts, just preparation.

Okay, enough thinking. Olympic Trials came, with or without the journeys of the mind. My parents and other family members usually didn't travel to my big meets with the exception of the Olympics, when my dad and grandpa came to Seoul. My mother would almost become ill at even the smallest meets because of her nerves, so she would stay home and maybe get to see the meet on TV. The 1992 Olympic Trials was a big exception. Both my mom and my dad drove from Albuquerque to Baltimore to be present at this meet. They told me they had two reasons. One was that my birthday would come during Trials. The other was that they felt my chances of making team were slim, and they wanted to be there to support me. They had seen first-hand what a great struggle it had been for me to fight back from my injury. They had no expectations, but they wanted to be there for me. That's family! They had been there when I started gymnastics, and they wanted to be there to celebrate the completion of that long and wonderful journey. They came, they sat, and they watched, and I loved them for it.

The first event for me (big surprise) was pommel horse. I hit a very strong compulsory routine and was off to a great start. Rings was my second event, and with a solid horse set behind me, I was much more relaxed. It was in my head to try not to bend my arms as I completed the iron cross this time. I did not want to sacrifice those points I had given away at Nationals for bending them, even if it meant more pressure on my shoulder. I started my set very strong, and when I got to the cross, I had only a slight arm bend as I transitioned out of it. I finished my routine very well, and I was happy with the outcome. I had to wait awhile for my score, though, because the judges had a conference to talk about my set. My coach wasn't sure what the problem was, though he thought I might not have held the cross long enough. I could not recall how long I had held it because I had been so focused on doing the transition with straight arms. Finally the judges posted my score. It was a very disappointing 8.9. I had scored a 9.6 at Nationals, so this was a dramatic drop. At a competition of this level, a gymnast could not get such a low score and hope to make the team. The judges' controversy continued, and they ended up deducting the full value of the cross from my routine. This was devastating. I had only completed my second event, and my hopes of a second Olympic team berth were nearly crushed. There was nothing I could do but go event to event and finish the meet, doing my very best. The next four routines of the day were incredibly strong for me. After all, I felt I had nothing to lose, so the pressure dynamic had changed for me. I went from being favored to being an underdog in one routine. . .in one decision of the judges.

That night, I thought about my rings routine over and over. Many of the coaches I spoke with that night said the judges could have gone either way as it was questionable as to how long I had held the cross. Little did I know at the time that this questionable judgment call would change the way future Olympic gymnastics teams would be chosen for the United States.

I was in eighth place after the first day of competition. This was much better than expected, given that extremely low score on rings. I had to move up to the top seven places to be named to the Olympic team, and among the top seven, only six would compete in the Olympic Games. I had my work cut out for me in the optionals. If I had been at full strength, doing my normally difficult routines, I would be sitting pretty to make the team. But, with the exclusion of some of my more difficult skills that were hard on my shoulder, things were up in the air for me.

The next morning came quickly, and this was the day the Olympic team would be named. The first three events I was to compete on were floor, pommel horse and rings. (I almost wished I could start on pommels—NOT!) Floor was very solid. Pommel horse was solid as well, and it was a huge relief to have it behind me. Then it was time for rings. I performed the iron cross, and I held it an extra couple of seconds so there would be absolutely no doubt that I was more than capable of performing that skill. It was one of the best routines I had done since my injury, and I scored almost a point higher than I had scored on the previous day. Although I felt vindicated on rings, I was still playing catch up in the competition. I was still in eighth place after rings, and the competition was close. As is always the case for Trials, everybody was in great shape, and everyone wanted a place on that team.

My next event was high bar. This was my strongest event, and being a former world champion on this event would work in my favor if I hit. I would be performing the very same routine that won me that title. Once again, it included a lot of difficulty but also a lot of risk. I rocked every skill in the routine and stuck my landing. My score was a nearly perfect 9.95! After the high bar, I moved up to a solid seventh place. If I could just maintain my momentum and hit my last two events, I would be named to the 1992 Olympic team.

No pressure.

Vault was next. It was strong. I could have landed with a smaller hop, but I scored well and stayed in seventh place. My last event was the parallel bars. I had to make cutbacks on my difficulty, and although I was still strong on this event, I was not the bronze medalist I had been before. I got through my routine; it was very clean and solid. I had to wait and see what the judges decided. I had done my job, and I felt good about that. There was a very long conference among the judges again. It was extremely difficult to wait. I was one of three gymnasts who was on what is called the 'bubble,' waiting for that last place on the team. The other two had received their last scores, and we were all waiting for mine.

Waiting. Waiting. Waiting.

My score was finally posted, but I still didn't know if it was enough to put me in the top seven. Across the gym, I saw one of the gymnasts awaiting the outcome celebrating, and that made me think I had not made the team. Then, I was asked on camera by the TV network commentator if I wanted to know if I had made the team. Did I want to know? I said, "Yes," of course, and she told me right there that I had made the 1992 Olympic team, and I was headed for Barcelona, Spain! In a matter of seconds, all that I had been through in the previous nine months and all that I had overcome hit me hard, and I could not contain the tears. All I wanted to hear was that I was an Olympian again, and to hear it almost made me jump out of my skin. I was so totally happy. I would be the seventh man on the U.S. team. Although that meant I was the alternate, and that I would only compete if somebody else was not able to, I was still a two-time Olympian, and that would never be taken away.

Like the feeling of a first kiss, the feeling I had four years before when I was eighteen and qualified for the Olympics could never be replaced. But this time, it was different. It was much more. It was deeper. All that I had overcome—the pain, the limits, and the doubts—made this second Olympic team sweeter and so very appreciated. The media kept asking me if I was disappointed being the seventh man on the team. I responded that to me, it was a miracle that I was even at the Trials. If I had come into the competition in perfect health and in the optimal shape that I was usually in, I would have been disappointed not to be in the top three. Some didn't understand my attitude. But if they had known all that I had been through in the previous nine months, they would have understood me much better. It was okay; I understood me.

Chapter 11

DEEP THOUGHTS, AND THE '92 OLYMPICS

I was always different from my fellow competitors. I liked training more than I liked competition. I do believe that competition brings out the best ability in a person, but I just loved to train. Even among my fellow gymnasts, I think I had and still have one of the most unceasing, child-like loves for the sport of gymnastics. The feeling of flying and of getting stronger and stronger was always at the core of my gymnastics. Everyday of training was a challenge, and there was and is a unique momentum in training. I loved trying to learn new skills that made me feel like a more powerful superhero. The world of training is different from that of competition, and both worlds have their pros and cons. What I lacked in being an aggressive competitor, I made up for with the intense training that served me well in competition. I was always much more philosophical than most of my friends. I believed then and still believe that being the best at something was not the same as being the best person I could be. The idea of cause and effect has a lot of value to me. I realized a long time ago that every word and every action in my life has the potential to affect someone, and I have always hoped it would be for the good. Most of us will live to be a grand old age and the effect we have on the world around us is what I believe has the greatest power, so we need to make it good.

These thoughts have become tangible to me many times over. For instance, there was a kid who saw me win a gold medal in 1990, and because of that, he began taking gymnastics classes. That kid went on to become an Olympic gymnast in 1996, competing for the U.S. That was very cool. His name is Brett McClure, and when I found out about his story, it really impacted me. Because of things like that, I do believe that life is about other people's lives. I reached the level of gymnastics that I did not only because of my dedication to and love for the sport, but also because of the people around me. The other athletes who gave me advice even in passing and with whom I trained radically affected my gymnastics. Because of those athletes, I learned skills and new techniques, and sometimes I even developed new philosophies that helped me to perform better. My teammates, even in the bad times, always made me a better gymnast. We were all better because of each other. We pushed each other, if not by encouragement all the time, by just being in the gym together. And, in 1992, we pushed each other right to the Olympic Games in Barcelona.

The qualifying procedure for the Olympics was different in 1992 from what it is today. Now, the Olympic team is picked from the top ten gymnasts at the Trials, so if a gymnast happens to be in tenth place after Trials but he is strong on a certain event, a committee can pick him to be on the Olympic team. The reason for this is to highlight and utilize the specialists in the world of gymnastics. A specialist is a gymnast who does not compete on all six events. Instead, he only does the events he is exceptionally strong in. He may only do two events, but if he has a chance at a medal, or if his score would help the team score a lot on his specialty, he may be placed on the Olympic team. This allows gymnasts to stay in the sport much longer than they used to be able to. The peak of a career for a male gymnast is typically when he is in his early to mid-twenties. Now, with event specialists, it is possible to see a few gymnasts who only train on one or two events compete even into their early thirties. In 1992, the top seven athletes at the Olympic Trials made up the Olympic team, and that could not be changed.

Every gymnast had to qualify on all the events, so if someone was weak on one event, he likely did not qualify for the Olympics.

Another difference, or change, is that we had two sets of routines in '92: compulsories and optionals. Presently, gymnasts only do the optionals, so this has, in some ways, cut the workload of a gymnast in half. The result, with the specialists and half the workload of the old days, is that there is now a very high level of gymnastics in the world. The difficulty has gotten much higher than it was for the Olympians of '92, because gymnasts can focus on one or two events only. There aren't as many ironman all-arounders who excel on all the events. There is still an individual event all-around final at the Olympics, but many of the gymnasts do not compete all-around in the Olympics anymore.

So, back to my gymnastics. I had made the '92 Olympic team, and once again, after a week or two at home to train and get ready to travel to Barcelona, Spain, the Olympic team met in Indianapolis for the training camp. It was very much the same as it had been for the '88 Olympics. We trained for around three hours in the morning and three hours in the afternoon. The team was close, and we wanted to have a much better showing than we had in Seoul, so we were motivated.

Just as in 1988, the U.S. team went through processing a day before leaving for Barcelona. Going through processing is still among my coolest of memories. Processing was when we got all the "stuff" the sponsors contributed, along with the U.S. uniforms we would march out in during opening ceremonies and during the competition itself. I still have a lot of that really cool stuff after going through those two processes. Like the first time around, I was provided with Olympic leather jackets, underwear, sunglasses, suits – anything one could think of that people might need if they were to go to Barcelona with nothing. It was an amazing experience.

Once we arrived in Spain, we were taken to the Olympic village to get checked in and to get our credentials. The village was awesome; it had three beaches within the village limits. Our dorm rooms were very nice, and we all stayed in an apartment setting again. I loved the village atmosphere, with the excitement, the level of talent and dedication that was everywhere, and the chance to get to know athletes from all over the world. One of the best things for me was to see the Soviet gymnasts again. I was good friends with many of them by this time, and it was great to be with them again in such a great place. On one occasion, their team was talking to one of our coaches who told me they were laughing at the fact that the U.S. had placed one of their best gymnasts in the position of reserve. That was very flattering to me. Although I trained and prepared just as all the U.S. team members did, I was indeed in the reserve position, so I would only compete if somebody else on the team was unable to. The Soviets had a different system; whoever was performing best on the days preceding the Olympics would compete for their team. The United States did not do it that way at that time. Though I was established internationally and still considered the top U.S. contender, I had finished Trials in the reserve spot. The United States changed their rules for the next Olympics, adopting the Soviet system to choose the gymnasts that they thought would contribute the best to the U.S. team. Not so in '92, but regardless of the system, the goal for the U.S. has always been to put the best possible team up against the other countries.

Training at the Olympics was fun for me. The U.S. was a much better team than it had been in 1988, so I was hopeful for a better showing for us. I was a bit disappointed to not be competing, but being a reserve took the pressure off of me, and I really got to soak up the Olympic experience in real time. I still had to train and be in top shape, and I was, but I really enjoyed the Olympics in a much different way than I had during my first experience back in 1988. After all, I could do nothing about being the reserve, and I was already feeling nostalgic about this Olympics because I did not know what could happen during the next four years before the '96 Olympics. So, I took it all in, and I enjoyed it to the fullest.

By the way, after I qualified for the 1992 Olympic team, I learned that sponsors would again be helping two family members of each athlete to attend the Olympics in Barcelona. My mom, who still chose not to fly, would not be going, and my dad had gone in 1988, so it was decided that my mom's parents, Nana and Earl, would travel to Barcelona. There are some important things to note about Earl before I continue. When he was young, he played baseball in the minor leagues, and he was just a huge fan of sports in general. Anytime there were high-level sports on TV, he would watch intensely. For years, even decades, he followed the players' stats and performances in all different sports. For him to be able to go to the Olympics and be around all these great athletes and sports was just incredible for Earl. He behaved like a kid in a candy store. Nana was more laid back about sports, but she understood how much of a sports fan Earl was, and she really enjoyed seeing him so excited about going to the Olympics. In addition to the gymnastics events, Earl went to see many of the other sports competitions. And, of course, many of the Olympic athletes were present at a reception to which families, including Nana and Earl, were invited. Nana had a wonderful time with the parents of the other athletes, and Earl looked like a ping-pong ball bouncing from great athlete to great athlete, taking pictures and having conversations. For that entire time, he laughed and smiled. Once again, for me to see my grandparents experience such a great event and to have such a wonderful time was incredibly fulfilling for me. Just like my dad and grandpa after 1988, for the next several years after the 1992 Olympics, Nana and Earl spoke often of their many experiences shared at the Olympics in Barcelona.

Of course, we were there for the competition, so let's get back to that. The Olympic competition went on in much the same way as it did in 1988. The Soviets, who were called the Unified Team at this point, still were the team to beat. Although they were not as strong as they had been in '88, they still dominated the medals. The U.S. also did very well though, with only a few mistakes here and there. We finished in fifth place all around. We might have had a shot at a bronze if we had not made those mistakes, but it would have been close either way. We did make a statement that the U.S. was on the rise again. Our biggest highlight was the gold medal performance of Trent Dimas, my teammate from Gold Cup in Albuquerque, on the high bar. We were all thrilled to see that happen; it was a great moment for the United States.

The competition concluded, and we had the rest of the Olympics to hang out and just enjoy our experience. We rented bikes and rode around the village. We went to a lot of the other sports venues and watched the games. We just enjoyed the atmosphere, and because we all got along so well, we just enhanced each other's experience of the Olympics in general. The team went many places and spent a lot of time together. Meeting the other athletes from the different sports was great. It is only at the Olympics that athletes really get a chance to meet great athletes from other sports. It was kind of funny, because on many occasions, I would be very honored to meet a great athlete, and to my surprise, other athletes would act like they were honored to meet me. We all respected each other for what we had gone through to get to the Olympics and for our accomplishments.

The closing ceremonies were incredible and very meaningful for us all. None of us wanted the experience to end, and we sincerely appreciated every moment of it. After the closing ceremonies, we all flew back to the U.S. and to our respective homes, scattered around the country. But soon, the Olympians from the 1992 Games were invited to the White House. This was my third invitation. I was much more appreciative of this event in 1992 than I had been in 1988. I was so young in 1988 that I was a bit oblivious. In '92, I was more aware of what an honor it was to be invited. I was also more aware of the work and dedication that went into accomplishing the things that would lead to such honors. Basically, I was just more appreciative that things had worked out for me the way that they had at that point in my career. President George H. W. Bush was in office at that time, and just as we had done in 1988, we shook hands and received words of congratulations and encouragement from the President.

For the next few months following the Olympics, we all got together as the Olympic team to go on a gymnastics tour. We went from city to city, performing exhibitions for large audiences, just as we had done in 1988. In 1988, though, we had only been to a few cities, and in 1992, we went to twenty-three. The tour was run by "Bill Graham Presents," and it was run very smoothly. In fact, "Bill Graham Presents" had previously run tours for groups like *Metallica, Guns 'n Roses,* and *The Grateful Dead.* They knew what they were doing, so the tours were a lot of fun for all of us. Just like the other tours, there was no pressure. We got to share our sport with the country, and we just enjoyed performing for the audiences. We also got paid for touring; that was a nice perk.

Many of the Soviet athletes were on this tour as well, so we trained together and just got to know more about each other. It was really interesting and intriguing, learning how they trained. The tour was in the U.S., and the Soviets loved being in our country. It was on this tour that the Soviets taught me to speak enough Russian to get by, and I helped them with their English—"Lance English!" None of us really thought about the next season. We were all just living in the moment: training, performing, and enjoying the experience.

The last city of the tour was Albuquerque, New Mexico—my home. This was the highest note on which to end the tour for me.

After battling my way back from injury, after making a second Olympic team, after living out my dreams through my career, I got to perform for my home crowd. I got to just be me. I even got to sing! After performing a routine on high bar in the Albuquerque show, I picked up a microphone and went to town! People still comment on that. In fact, some people remember that more than they remember the high bar routine. Go figure.

I have one final thought about that tour and the stop in Albuquerque. While we were there, two of the Soviet athletes, one being Vitali Scherbo, 1992 Olympic champion, wanted to see my gym. I called my coach, Burch, to let him know we were coming, and he was so excited he could hardly speak. The kids at the gym were very excited to see the Soviet Olympians. Vitali was gracious enough to talk and sign autographs as well as help with a little coaching. It was a really nice thing they did. They were good friends to us, and their presence in the gym was proof that we are not all that different. Yes, we're worlds apart, but we love the same things, we train in the same sports, and we laugh when children are around.

Chapter 12

LAST DAYS OF COMPETITION

The 1992 Olympics were over, and the gymnastics tour came to an end. It was time for me to decide what I wanted to do in gymnastics. I knew what it took to maintain being world class, and I did not know if I could do that for another four years. Frankly, I didn't know if I wanted to. So, I just decided not to decide, and I trained very hard for the remainder of the summer just to have fun and because I loved the sport.

As the summer of '92 drew to a close and the next competitive season was beginning, I still had not given much thought as to whether I would continue training or competing in gymnastics. Winter Nationals were to be held at the Olympic Training Center in Colorado Springs, and as that was close to New Mexico, it was a possibility. Also, the top seven gymnasts at the Winter Nationals were paid based on how they ranked. It was enough money to support continued training without having to get a job. (FYI: Present day gymnasts make much more money based on their rank.) With all that in mind, I thought, "Why not go to Winter Nationals just to have some fun, to see many of my friends again, and to try to make some money?" I was in good shape, and I had put together some new routines just in case I decided to continue competing. So, I went to the meet. Most of the '92 Olympic team was not there, as it is a common practice to take a little more time off after the Olympics and train and decide what goals to set for the next one to four years. Also, many Olympians retire after the Olympics. It is hard to look out four years in advance to shoot for another Olympic team. I knew as much as anyone that anything can happen in that time in the way of injury, or in just other younger, more motivated gymnasts coming up the ranks to push the older ones out. But, I went to Colorado Springs, nonetheless.

My mindset was different for this competition. As far as I knew, this could have been my last competition, so I was very laid back and just wanted to enjoy it. I had a really good time there, and I also had a really good meet. I placed third in the all-around, I won some money, and I felt good about still doing some really good gymnastics. That feeling of having a great competition—setting out to accomplish a goal and then making it happen—is very intoxicating and addictive. I loved the feeling of success and being a good gymnast. Winter Nationals also served as the qualifying meet for the American Cup (the most prestigious international invitational in the U.S.), and for World Championships to be held in England at the end of the year. There was prize money at the American Cup as well as good TV coverage. It was a huge accomplishment to qualify for a World team and very hard to turn down. Much to my surprise, I qualified for both of these competitions.

So, I had gone to Winter Nationals undecided about the direction I would follow, and before I knew it, I had an entire season ahead of me again. I had mixed feelings about that. I just wanted to have fun for a while in the sport, but these competitions came with a great deal of pressure attached, and to train for them was very intense. My mind was not really ready for another season yet, but now, with qualifying, I had no choice but to get both my mind and my body ready.

I went back home and into the gym with a good attitude. I concentrated on trying to have fun with training and not to stress so much. The next meet was the American Cup. Even though this would be a major competition, I managed to stay pretty relaxed and casual in preparation. I trained incredibly hard, but mentally I had no expectations of myself, other than to simply do as I had trained. In my mind, my career was beginning to wind down. I just wanted it to be fun, and it was.

The American Cup was in Florida. We arrived there about three days before the competition to get acclimated to the equipment. It became almost overwhelming to see my old friends when I would go to a meet of this magnitude. I had known many of the other competitors from all around the world for years, and I had had many great times with them. It is like we had grown up together, so it was just cool to me to see how all of us had grown from inexperienced, young gymnasts to young men with confidence and world-class skill levels. Ironically, many of my friends from the other countries were also in the middle of deciding if they wanted to hang in there for another four years and try for the Olympics or not. I never even considered retiring after the '88 Olympics because I was so young, but apparently, after every Olympics, it is common to be faced with the decision about going on or not. After all, the Olympics is the peak of sport, and it is incredibly intense to work for another four years to make another team, with no guarantee of making it. That is why athletes have to truly love the sport. They just can't force themselves to do what is necessary to be world class if they don't have some kind of passion for the everyday involvement in the sport.

The American Cup required only the optional routines, which were more difficult, stronger routines for me. The field of gymnasts was headed up by the Russian gymnast, Vitali Scherbo. He was the 1992 Olympic Champion, holding six gold medals from that Olympics. (Vitali is also the man I tied in the Goodwill Games on high bar in 1990.) There were many Olympians from all around the world at the American Cup. Frankly, I thought there would be more new and younger gymnasts from other countries. But, it was a prize competition, so it was really no surprise that the best of the best showed up.

In warm-ups, I was very relaxed and almost playful in how I felt. At the same time, though, everything I did in gymnastics at this point was stirring up powerful feelings of nostalgia in me, for I knew I would miss being part of the wonderful world of elite gymnastics after I retired.

Once the competition started, I continued to feel relaxed and playful, and that was very odd for such a major competition. Event by event, I began and ended my routines as if I were training and just having fun. It was a televised competition, and I would look into the camera between events to say "hi" to family and friends. Somehow, in the process of having fun, I had a great competition. When the American Cup ended, I was second in the all-around, first place being awarded to Olympic Champion Vitali Scherbo. This was a huge surprise, and I was thrilled. I won some extra money, received television exposure, and just had a great time.

After the American Cup, as with all major meets, we had a reception for all the athletes and coaches. It was a time to talk and just chill with our fellow gymnasts. Many of the athletes I spoke with had decided to compete a year or two more, but could not commit to another four years at that point. I would say less than half the athletes planned to go on to the next Olympics. We all talked more about past competitions than we did about future competitions, which was pretty telling about how our minds were working.

The year after every Olympics, the rules change. More difficulty is required, new trends are introduced, and routines have to be changed and improved in order to stay competitive. If a gymnast lacks motivation to change with the sport, he will gradually fall in the rankings. After the American Cup, I had about four months before the World Championships. During this time, my coach and I added new skills to my sets and constructed new combinations that would score well with the new rules. This was a difficult time for me because I still did not know what I wanted to do with my sport. The only bad thing about being a world-class gymnast is that at that level, gymnasts cannot do much of anything else. They have to train all the time to stay strong and competitive with the rest of the world, and doing that is a full time commitment. I had always wanted to start my own gymnastics program, where I could teach little kids in daycare centers, but as long as I was training, such a thing was not possible. I felt divided between continuing competition and doing other things I had wanted to do for a while. "Divided" is not the way to be when training to stay world class. If one is not one hundred percent dedicated, then it is not enough. I recognized that, but I still had to get ready for World Championships in England. I felt that the 1993 Worlds could be my last competition, but I did not want to commit to a decision yet. The truth is, I still didn't really have to.

World Championships in Birmingham were different from other Worlds. Only four gymnasts per country could qualify, and that was different from the usual seven. But remember, flexibility is the key in gymnastics! So, four of us were prepared for the World Championships.

After getting settled in our hotel in England, the U.S. team went to the gym for our workout. We had about three days before the actual meet to get used to the time change and equipment. As the top sixty countries were represented, there were a lot of athletes. It was cool to see the new faces and to see how everyone was changing the routines to fit the new rules.

Training went very well for me, but I was tired from the flight so I just took it pretty slow the first day. The whole team did, actually. I was more interested in watching the other gymnasts train than I was in training myself. Anytime I could see new, innovative and live gymnastics, it was a great plus. I was also just soaking up what I knew might be my last major competition. I felt more like an observer than a participant at this meet, which was a strange dynamic.

The days of training passed, and it was finally competition day. Event by event, the meet progressed. I got through my routines, but I had a couple of major breaks on some new skills I was trying out, meaning they did not go as well as I had hoped they would. I remember thinking that each event could be my last in competition, which put a poignant spin on things. It was not going badly for me, but I was not doing nearly the level I was capable of doing and I could feel that my drive was not what it should be. To be successful, a gymnast has to have a fire in his soul and a desire that rules over everything else. I had had that kind of strong drive for thirteen years as a competitor, but at this meet, it just wasn't there. I did very well on events like high bar and floor exercise, but I was slightly out of the medals.

Even without a medal, I finished the competition with nostalgia, appreciation, and peace about my entire career. It felt like the end, but it did not make me sad. My gymnastics career flashed through my mind as I thought about all that I had achieved. There were so many great memories that I just had a good feeling about everything. And, despite the conclusion I was feeling, I knew I still had choices. They were either to retire completely or to take some significant time off from the sport and see how I felt after that. I decided I would wait until I got back home and played in the gym for a while to see how I felt and to make a final decision. No matter what the future held, I would take home great memories from England. I had enjoyed my stay very much, and I had spent most of my time with gymnastics friends from all over the world.

Photo Gallery

LANCE'S FIRST BACK HANDSPRING, AGE 9

LANCE'S FIRST GYMNASTICS TEAM
CEDAR RAPIDS, IOWA, 1980
(Lance is on the far left)

LANCE IN TRAINING, 1985

MAKING THE OLYMPIC
TEAM, 1988

LANCE AT THE SEOUL OLYMPICS, 1988

To Lance Ringnald
With best wishes, *G. Bush* *Barbara Bush*

LANCE MEETING PRESIDENT AND MRS. GEORGE H.W. BUSH, 1988

LANCE WITH GOOD FRIEND AND TEAMMATE, DOMINICK MINICUCCI
BARCELONA OLYMPICS, OPENING CEREMONIES, 1992

CELEBRATING VICTORY

LANCE RELAXING IN BARBADOS

LANCE'S OWN TRICK—A MALTESE ON PARALLEL BARS

LANCE PERFORMING ON HIS FIRST CRUISE SHIP, 1995

LANCE'S ACROBATIC SKILLS ON SILKS

MORE OF LANCE'S ARTISTRY ON SILKS

LANCE IN TEXAS WITH HIS PARENTS AND HIS BROTHER, JOE

Chapter 13

LIFE AFTER COMPETITION

Once I got home from World Championships in England, I went into the gym and trained really hard everyday. I did not think about competition at all or what I wanted to do in the world of gymnastics. I just did it for fun. There was no doubt that I loved to train, and I loved the sensation that gymnastics gave me of flying and feeling so strong and being in such great shape. Basically, I loved doing gymnastics. So, while my mind was unsettled, I just concentrated on that.

Since I was undecided about whether or not I would continue to compete, I decided to finally start my own gymnastics business while I continued to train. It was something I had thought about throughout my competitive years, but I was always much too busy with training to pursue it. This seemed like a good time to give it a go.

I called my gymnastics program "Gym Kids." I loaded a bunch of small gymnastics equipment and mats into a trailer, and I took it to different pre-schools and daycare centers around the city. It was a mobile gym! I set up a little gymnastics area with the equipment at the daycare, and a couple of other former gymnasts and I taught kids ages three to ten basic gymnastics. The kids signed up through the daycare, and with little or no overhead for me, it was a great deal. I had fun, and the kids had fun. At the end of the first year, I had one hundred fifteen kids in my program. I loved teaching that age of children because they were very excited to flip around, and they seemed to enjoy learning new skills. Everything was new to them at that age, and they learned very quickly. Also, I remembered my vivid imagination and my desire to be a superhero when I was young, and I could see that same imagination in some of my students.

I still did not know what I wanted to do with competitive gymnastics, but I was not thinking about it much at that time. I was just enjoying training, trying to learn new tricks, and building my "Gym Kids" gymnastics business. Although I continued to train every day and stay in very good shape, I decided to take the next season off from competition and concentrate exclusively on "Gym Kids". Well, not exclusively. During this period, I also traveled occasionally to other gymnastics programs around the country to do clinics and camps and some coaching, and I did the occasional public speaking engagement or exhibition, but I was home for my business most of the time. I really liked that. It felt like normal life.

After the first year, my business had grown larger and I needed someone reliable to run Gym Kids when I traveled to other gymnastics engagements. I found this reliable person in my good friend, Stacey Lake. She was a former gymnast from Gold Cup; I met her there when I first moved to Albuquerque in 1985. A year or two after we met, she had to quit gymnastics because of an injury. But later, she had become a coach of gymnastics at a local YMCA. We had stayed in touch through the years, and I had done exhibitions and talked to her YMCA students occasionally. Stacey was looking for more coaching opportunities, so I hired her to help me with Gym Kids. Whenever I was out of town (which would be a little more often over time) I knew that Gym Kids would be in good hands, and Stacey was very happy with the position. From 1993, after the World Championships, until 1995, I focused on my Gym Kids business, I trained five days each week, and I traveled around the country giving gymnastics clinics and speeches. It was good. It was really good. And, though I hadn't ever really made a formal decision, apparently I had "retired" from gymnastics competition, and I was OK with that. The decision just sort of made itself.

MY FIRST PERFORMANCE ON A CRUISE SHIP

In 1995, I got a call from Kurt Thomas, 1976 Olympic gymnast and former American gymnastics icon. The world of gymnastics is pretty small, and I knew Kurt from a gymnastics tour I had previously done. When he called, he was starring in a gymnastics show on Norwegian Cruise Lines, and he wanted to know if I could replace him for a few weeks while he took a break. He knew that I was in transition in my gymnastics career, and he thought I might be available and a good fit to replace him. To me, this seemed to be a great adventure, and the job paid well. I also knew my business, Gym Kids, would be just fine with Stacey running it, so I decided to go.

Norwegian Cruise Lines flew me to meet up with Kurt on the *Norwegian Windward*, which was sailing in Alaska at the time. Kurt had one week to teach me what he did in the show. I had no idea what to expect when I got there. I had never been on a cruise ship before, but I had heard that they were very big. I had heard correctly, because when I arrived, I found it to be a small, floating city. I quickly learned that I would be doing tumbling, rings, pommel horse and mini-tramp in the show. It was a gymnastics show built around a gymnast and accompanied by a cast of ten singers and dancers. I basically came out and did some short gymnastics routines in-between the singers and dancers doing their numbers. I was in really good shape, so it was not hard to do the gymnastics. It was a challenge, however, to tumble on a floor that would sometimes be swaying with a rough sea! It was also a challenge to learn how to count music and to time everything around the other performers. That was a new experience for me. The cast was very welcoming to me, though, and they helped me fit into the show smoothly.

After a week of rehearsals with the cast and Kurt showing me what to do in the show, it was time for me to open my first cruise ship show. The opening went great, and I could tell I would enjoy the four weeks I would be spending there.

LIFE ON THE CRUISE SHIP

Entertainers are pretty spoiled on a cruise ship. I only worked a couple of days each week, and I had all the privileges of a paying passenger. Of course, the true passenger always comes first, but I had great perks. I was housed in a passenger cabin, and I got paid for going on cruises. It was all such a new experience for me: seeing Alaska, which I grew to love, entertaining with the skills I had already developed during much of my younger life, enjoying the atmosphere of a beautiful cruise ship, and getting paid well to do it. It was all new to me, but it also seemed very natural for me. I felt much less pressure as an entertainer gymnast than I had as a competitive gymnast. The crowds judged me much less harshly than I was used to being judged in competition. That was a nice change.

Kurt Thomas returned to the ship, and my first cruise ship experience came to an end. I remember telling Kurt, "Thanks a lot for the opportunity. I had a great time, and if you ever decide to move on and do something else other than the ships, I would love to come and replace you on a more permanent basis."

Be careful what you wish for. . .

I went home and continued to train and teach in my own business. About four months after I had replaced Kurt on the ship, he called me and asked me if I wanted to come replace him on the ship again—on a more permanent basis. He had decided to go to Texas and open a gymnastics school. I was more than happy to go back on the ship, and once again, Stacey had no problem running Gym Kids while I was away. I met the ship in the Caribbean this time, as it had repositioned from Alaska a couple of months earlier. The Caribbean was beautiful. The shows were the same, so I had no problem picking up right where I had left off four months prior. When I arrived on the ship, most of the people I had worked with when I was there before were still there, so I even had friends there already. I signed a six-week contract. At the time, a common length for a cruise ship contract was six months, but because I was a specialty act in the show, I had more flexibility of how short or long my contracts could be.

I was the star of the production show, <u>Sea Legs: Circus at Sea</u>. I did cameos, or short little appearances, in the other two production shows, and the other nights of entertainment were filled with guest entertainers. A guest entertainer was usually someone who did his or her own fifty-minute show. It might be a singer, a world champion juggler, a comedian, or a TV personality. I got to meet all kinds of great performers and learn about the world of entertainment. I was offered many more contracts on the ship. I continued doing the ship job for a few years, off and on, but during the off times, I would go home and teach at Gym Kids or do an occasional gymnastics clinic or exhibition.

Life continued to take me on new adventures and all around the world on cruise ships. But, in 1996, I took some time off and worked for the international television coverage of the 1996 Olympic Games held in Atlanta, Georgia. My heart—my passion—was always with gymnastics, and being around the Olympics again, though I was not competing, was a huge high for me. A couple of my other Olympic teammates were working for TV in Atlanta also, so it was a gymnastics reunion. It was really good to be around the gymnastics world again.

As I said before, I never formally decided to retire from gymnastics competition. I just simply started doing other things, and life took on a whole different dimension for me. I did not miss competition, but I did miss the people in the world of gymnastics and being part of something that felt so special to be a part of. Being at the Olympics in Atlanta reminded me of that. But, I had a lot of peace in my life. And, when I wasn't on a cruise ship, I was still training everyday in the gym and coaching, so I still got to do and be around gymnastics.

I got to be part of gymnastics in a big way in the year 2000. Every couple of years, the U.S. Gymnastics Federation organizes a competition that is based on gymnastics entertainment as well as gymnastics ability. In 2000, Reese's sponsored this competition, and it was called the Reese's Cup. It was televised, and it featured the most recognized Olympic and World Class gymnasts at the time. A year before this competition, I sent a video of my routines to the head of the USGF, showing him some ideas I had for the possibility of my competing in the Reese's Cup. Yes, it had been a long time since I was in the Olympics, but I was still training everyday, and I had stayed in very good shape. The training paid off, because although it had been six years since my last national competition, the head of the USGF liked what he saw and decided to invite me to this meet. After all, since my last gymnastics competition, I had become an entertainer, and I used gymnastics as my vehicle to entertain. That's what the Reese's Cup was trying to promote.

With this invitation, once again, I had a challenge to meet. This drove me to train very hard. I was a very experienced competitor, and I had become somewhat experienced in the world of entertainment, but this type of combined competition/entertainment was unlike anything I had ever done. In the competition, we had to do two events. For each of those two events, we had to choose a theme or develop a kind of skit to incorporate with our routine. We were going to be judged on gymnastics difficulty, on entertainment value, and on how well we were received by the audience. All the judges were celebrity judges, and the competition was designed to be entertaining. Serious stuff.

The other competitors were going to give me a run for my money—that was certain. They included the Olympic Champion Alexei Nemov from Russia, U.S. Olympians Paul and Morgan Hamm, and John Roethlisberger, who was not only the five-time NCAA champion but also a three-time Olympian by this point. The field also included many other Olympic and World champions, male and female, from both the U.S. and Russia. It was going to be quite an event.

For my floor exercise routine, I chose to impersonate Axl Rose, the lead singer of the rock band "Guns and Roses." They allowed me to use a microphone on floor, and I entered fully clad as Axl, singing a Guns and Roses song. As the tempo of the music changed, I went into my tumbling passes. Halfway through my routine, I incorporated a sing-along of the Bob Dylan classic, "Knocking on Heaven's Door." An arena of seven thousand people enthusiastically sang along as they echoed each phrase I sang! The energy was incredible, and everyone had a great time during this routine— myself included. After I finished my last tumbling pass, I waited for my scores to be posted. My mix of difficult tumbling passes and a rocked out sing-along proved to be innovative and ground breaking, not to mention successful. My score was a perfect 10!

Lest you get as excited as I did, keep in mind that this was not a conventional competition; it was based on skill and entertainment value. Therefore, scoring was much more liberal than normal. Even so, I was thrilled with my score.

After floor, I went on to my second event, high bar, where I was a court jester, wearing a great costume my mom had made for me. I incorporated some juggling, and I walked the high bar as if it were a tight rope. I also created a skill for this competition in which I straddled my feet to the sides and slid down into a center split on the bar, then I swung around the bar in the split position. This new skill received a great response from the audience, as it had never been done before, and it looked both fun and difficult.

It was fun, and it required tremendous flexibility. I was glad I still maintained that. I finished the routine with a series of full twisting giant swings into a full twisting back fly away to a perfect landing. Once again, the originality and innovation proved to be well worth the effort, and the crowd and judges loved it. I scored a perfect 10 once again!

As my second score was revealed, I realized that I had captured the men's all-around gold medal, tying with Olympic Champion Alexei Nemov. The head of the U.S. Gymnastics Federation was extremely happy that he had taken a chance on me, and so was I! It was like another Olympics for me, in a way, and it was extremely rewarding because I achieved the goal I had set out to achieve. I had had the time of my life, and after not competing at all for six years, it just felt completely gratifying to be a part of such a great event and to do so well. It also felt good to apply some of the skills I had learned on the ships as an entertainer. I used those "entertainer" techniques in my gymnastics routines, and I got a great response from the audience. It was the perfect type of competition for me, and one I will never forget.

Chapter 14

THE NEED FOR NEW CHALLENGES

I had a LOT of free time while working on ships. When first starting cruise ship work, I was not used to all the extra time. Not at all. Once I learned and performed the shows for a few weeks, I didn't have to concentrate on them as much. I only worked two or three times each week, and that was only for a few hours in the evening. The rest of the time was all mine. Going from teaching gymnastics and training everyday to having all this free time made me go a little crazy (probably typical for an Olympic athlete). I knew I had to get into something or find something to challenge my mind, or I really would be nuts. So, I decided I should use that new free time as working and learning time for me. That was what I needed—a new challenge. So, I looked for other ways to use my time in a learning capacity. As soon as I started looking, I found that there were many new things to learn, and that's what drove me. I have always been driven by challenges and by learning. I am amazed at how discontented and restless I can get, even today, if I am missing those driving forces. But with them, the sky is once again the limit.

SILKS

After a few years of contracts on cruise ships, Jean Ann, the producer of the show I was starring in, called me up and asked if I wanted to star in a different gymnastics show on a different and larger ship. I was very happy on the ship I was on, but I also felt that a new challenge would be good for me. So, I agreed to do the new show. I went to rehearsals in Ft. Lauderdale, Florida. The show consisted of eighteen cast members, and just as I had done on my first ship, I would go on stage and do my solo routine, and I would also blend in with the cast for other parts of the show. Upon arrival at rehearsal, Jean Ann informed me that she would like me to learn these new things called "silks" that she had seen in a Cirque du Soleil show. She said they were like the gymnastics rings. I knew nothing about silks, and I had no idea what to expect. When I walked into the rehearsal area, I saw two long white pieces of fabric, twenty feet long, hanging from ceiling to floor. Actually, it was all one piece of fabric that was looped around at the top. They were called silks, but they were made out of tricot. I looked at these things with no idea what I was supposed to do on them. Jean Ann may have thought they were like gymnastics rings, but to me, they were long hanging bed sheets. She handed me a video of a silk-worker and told me to watch it to get some ideas of what I could do on the silks. I said I would take a look and give it a try, but I was very unsure if I could do it. Jean Ann wanted silks in the show, but she said that if I could not do it, she was fine not to have them. I had two weeks of rehearsal in Florida and another two weeks of rehearsal on the ship before we opened the show, so I felt I had enough time.

That night at the hotel, I looked over the silks video Jean Ann had given me. It showed a man who did mostly basic stuff on silks, with some splits and some flying, but he made it look very aesthetic. More importantly to me, the video gave me many ideas of how I could use my gymnastics ability to transfer on the silks. The next day, I started playing on the silks and trying things. Again, my obsessive passion kicked in. Everyday, after our normal rehearsal, I played around on the silks and tried new skills. Sometimes, I got caught up in the silks and nothing would work out right. Other times, I tried a gymnastics move and it would work great. It was trial and error for me. I had no teacher other than a very basic video. I later got another video of a different silks routine. That helped a lot. Basically, I tried what I saw on the video, and in doing so, other ideas of what gymnastics skills to try came about.

The routine Jean Ann was hoping for was supposed to be six minutes long. On stage, that is a long time. I was glad for lots of extra rehearsal time. In fact, I had three weeks before the entire cast flew to Bremen, Germany, where the ship was. It was a brand new ship called the *Norwegian Sky*. It was in dry dock, and they were just finishing up its construction when we arrived. Everyday, the cast and I would rehearse on the stage where we would eventually perform. This was very helpful in setting up spacing and getting a feel for our performance environment. And, it gave me more time to work on silks. My skills were coming along each day. Eventually, rehearsals were over, passengers all came aboard, and the ship left for America on its inaugural cruise. The cast was made up of many veterans of entertainment, because when a new ship came out, Jean Ann always tried to get the very best performers. They were all great at what they did.

By the time we opened the circus show in which I was the star, I had put together enough silks skills to fill a six-minute routine. I also did a short routine on some mini-parallel bars, and I did mini-tramp, tumbling, and pommel horse in the show. On those, of course, I was very experienced, so they were no problem. It was silks that were new to me, and although I had enough time to put together a six-minute routine, it was not nearly enough time to put together the skill level I would have liked. For as unconventional as my learning the silks was up to this point, I felt like there was a lot of potential there, and I was really enjoying them. I knew I would continue to train on them, and I was excited to learn more skills—even if it was after we opened the show. Despite my lack of skills at that point, opening night went really well, and the crowd seemed to like what I did. I felt really good about it, and I knew I would feel even better in the future.

In the months to come, I grew more and more passionate about silks. That was not a new feeling—it was one I have known for my entire life. If I find something I really enjoy, I do become passionate about it, and it absorbs my focus and my attention. I was that way about gymnastics, and now silks had me hooked. Every silks and circus video I could get my hands on, I watched and tried to learn from. I had some gymnast friends that were in <u>Cirque du Soleil</u> who told me how to train certain skills on the silks. I used any resource I could get to become better on these "hanging bed sheets." Over the next year, I came and went from that ship doing my gymnastics and silks performances. When I was home, off of the ship, I hung silks in the gym where I had trained for so many years and worked on them there as well. Burch, my coach, let me train in gymnastics and silks because I was an "Olympian," and because I would help coach at his gym sometimes. That was probably the real reason he let me hang around. By the end of the year, I had changed, added, and upgraded so much to my silks routine that it made my original silks routine look incredibly and almost embarrassingly amateurish. I felt that I had become a strong silks worker, and I really enjoyed feeling that I had accomplished another goal of mine. It also felt really good to know that I was using my free time productively. It was a new thing to learn, it was a challenge, and it allowed me to use a lot of the skills I already had in a brand new way.

PLAYING PIANO

I befriended many musicians during my first couple of stays on the ship. I liked hanging around them while they would jam. They were really talented, and they really seemed to enjoy their gifts. There was always a piano on stage, so I would sit down and play around on it between their rehearsals. I did not have a clue what I was doing, but it was fun anyway. Though it may have seemed like it to the professionals around me, those "play" sessions were not my first attempt at music, or at playing the piano. My brother grew up playing guitar and he was musically gifted, so I got some early exposure to music. I just never followed through with learning how to do it properly; I happily let gymnastics consume my life. Even so, before I started working on ships, I bought myself a keyboard and played around on it all the time. I also played around on the pianos in the daycare centers while waiting for my Gym Kids to come for their classes. It was still just "play," though. In fact, Stacey once laughed at me because I only played the "white" keys. I told her that I didn't think I should attempt playing the black keys when I didn't even know what I was doing. Stacey had to assure me that the "black" keys were just the same as the white ones; they each struck an individual note, and they all worked together to create the music. I still didn't quite get it, but even so, once I began cruising, I brought my keyboard along with me to the ship sometimes just so I could have something to do. I still never played much, though, because I really didn't know how.

One day when I was playing around on the piano on the ship's stage, a musician friend of mine sat down next to me and asked me if I would like to learn to play the piano. As strange as it sounds, I had never really thought about learning piano properly. I told him I would like to learn at least a little bit of piano just for fun and to stay busy. He knew I had a keyboard in my cabin, so he wrote down on some paper a few exercises I should start with, and he explained where my fingers should be properly placed on the keyboard. I pinned this piece of paper to my wall in my cabin and slowly, like a child, I learned to place my fingers on the keys one by one, as the paper instructed. I stumbled through my first major scales—*Do, Re, Mi, Fa, Sol, La, Ti, Do*—but I did them every day and got better and better. I would do one scale, and then I would modulate my fingers a half step up and practice the major scale in the next key. It was weird; I had to use the black keys along with the white keys! I would brashly stumble through my major scales in about three sessions each day for around twenty minutes or so. When I got bored, I sat down and just did these exercises. At first, my scale exercises would have made anybody laugh out loud, they were so bad, but each day they became more technically sound and natural to me.

The better I got at my exercises, the more fun it became and the longer I would practice. I showed my musician friend my progress after a couple of weeks, and he was very impressed. He drew up another paper for me showing minor scales and blues scales. Once again, I pinned them to the wall and practiced three times a day for about twenty minutes each time. Every couple of weeks, I would show him my progress, and he would write up more exercises and theory for me. The exercises became easier, and after I developed an understanding of how music works and how things fit together in the form of music theory, it was also much easier to play chords and scales in the theoretically correct way.

This routine of practicing went on for months, and the more I learned and the better I got at the piano, the longer I would play each day. In truth, I was hooked and just loved to play all the time. Again, my obsessive passion had kicked in. It got to the point that I was playing two and three hours each day because I enjoyed it so much. The same learning process I had developed for learning and perfecting my gymnastics skills transferred incredibly well to learning the piano.

Just as with silks, in learning to play the piano, I was discovering that the formula and techniques I was taught in my youth as a gymnast for learning new skills were helping me to learn anything I wanted much better and much more efficiently. My piano skills just increased more over time. I started listening to songs and learning how to play them. Once I had my basic chords and scales down, learning a song from listening to it became much easier. And, because I really enjoyed my newly developed piano skills, I was learning new songs all the time. Eventually, when the band would jam together, I would sit in on the piano and jam with them. Even if I did not know the song they were playing, they would tell me the key that the song was in and I could play along, just improvising with scales and chords. It was really cool to be able to sit in with a band and play music. I got very excited as I got better, and that excitement drove me to learn more and more on the piano.

After several months of practicing the piano between one and three hours a day, five to seven days a week, I had become a fairly proficient piano player. I was learning more, I was writing my own stuff, and I was finding incredible satisfaction in all of it. It was a great way to use my free time. Granted, I was not going to play jazz or classical very well, but for the average pop, rock, and mainstream music scene, I could hold my own. I even wrote a little "Rock Opera," with songs and lyrics designed to tell a story. It was a pretty powerful story, at least in my opinion. I had my friends on the ship help me record it, and I was really happy with the way it turned out. All of this has become yet another passion for me; I write and record music all the time now.

SINGING

As with so many other people, I always enjoyed singing while I was growing up. For most of my life, though, my best singing was pretty much confined to the shower and car. I became interested in the rock band "Guns and Roses" when I was a teenager, and I was really intrigued by the way Axl Rose, the lead singer, could sing. I used to drive all my friends crazy because I was always singing, or, they might say, screaming. I had a lot of energy, and to sing or scream helped me release much of that energy.

When I started my ship performance job, every night before I would do my production show on NCL, the cast would all warm up together. The dancers would stretch and the singers would do their vocal drills. I had my own stretch routine that I did while everybody else warmed up. When the singers started doing their vocal exercises, I would always do the exercises with them. The singers would tell me what to think about while doing these exercises. Sometimes I was told to produce a tone that would not blow a candle out if it were in front of me. Other times I would breathe and produce a tone that would definitely blow out a candle if it were in front of me. There were many exercises that helped me develop breath control, breath support, and tone to better hear if I was singing in key. I had enjoyed singing all my life, but now I was learning how to sing properly and how to get the most out of my voice. And, it became a fun thing to combine my new piano passion with singing, both for my own entertainment and for the entertainment of others.

JUGGLING

Continuing on with ship life, I enjoyed performing and visiting all the places the ship took me. I went to China, Australia, New Zealand, Germany, Canada, Mexico, the Caribbean Islands, Malaysia, Russia, and Scotland, to name a few. I felt very established in my role as an entertainer. I would meet many celebrities who would come on to do their own shows, and I really liked the variety of talent and personalities that I got to see. Comedians, musicians, singers, and jugglers were the most common guest entertainers.

I always liked it when juggling entertainers came on board. They were more like me in how they pursued their craft. Getting better and being challenged—those were their goals. I befriended many jugglers on ships and, of course, while hanging around them, I learned to juggle. When I was younger and in competitions, I used to juggle three balls in a few different patterns to clear my mind and to calm my nerves the night before a meet, so I already knew some basics. But, those basics were nothing compared to the level of the juggling that these guys did on ships. Many of them could juggle up to seven balls comfortably.

One of the jugglers who came on the ship from time to time was world champion juggler, Jason Garfield. We would often juggle together, but most of the time I would just watch him. He was incredible. He left me his "How to Juggle 3-11 Balls" teaching video on the ship after he left one contract, and with all my free time, I became obsessed with becoming a better juggler. Yes, it was once again that obsessive passion thing. I got so obsessed that I would juggle up to three hours a day. From Jason's video, I learned proper techniques and drills to better my juggling and once again, the art of learning was just like gymnastics to me. After about three months of this intense juggling, I finally mastered five balls. Most people who can catch a ball can learn three and four ball juggling pretty easily, with a little practice. Five-ball juggling is the major step, referred to as the level of black belt in juggling. The reason it is more difficult is that with five balls, there are three balls in the air at once, and they have to come down one at a time. If they do not, one cannot continue to juggle five balls. The pattern has to be perfect.

Once I mastered five-ball juggling, the sky was the limit because five-ball juggling is the foundation for everything beyond that. From watching Jason's video and practicing obsessively over a few years, I reached an elite level of juggling. I learned several patterns with five and six balls, and I became pretty solid with seven balls. I can now run eight balls for a very short time, and I have even flashed nine and ten balls on occasion. A flash is when jugglers throw all the balls up in the proper pattern once and then collect them all without dropping any.

Eventually, I grew accomplished enough as a juggler to be invited to perform a juggling and gymnastics exhibition in Las Vegas at a World Juggling Invitational. The invitational was hosted by Jason Garfield, the world champion juggler who had helped me to learn his art. He had arranged the competition, and he was also competing in it. It was hugely fulfilling to me to perform there, and I felt satisfied in the same way I had in gymnastics performances. It was that feeling of working hard to achieve something and finally, after all the time and work, reaching my goals. I did not want to become a competitive juggler, but to be invited to perform juggling and gymnastics at such a prestigious juggling event was great. Juggling was a small replacement for the challenges I used to have as a competing gymnast. I loved the challenge of it, and I loved growing better over time with training.

Chapter 15

DEVELOPING THE "LANCE RINGNALD SHOW"

T he more time I spent with the other guest entertainers, the more of my juggling, piano, and silks skills they saw, and the more they encouraged me to go out and do my own show. That would mean breaking away from being the highlighted gymnast in a group show and developing my own, full "Lance Ringnald" show. It was an intriguing idea, and there were lots of benefits attached to it. I would earn more money, I would have the freedom to do what I wanted in the show, I would have freedom with scheduling my time between home and the ship better, and I would have the freedom to actually speak while performing. That part would be really nice. I enjoyed the times I got to interact and connect with my audience, and that was definitely something I wanted more of.

This was all attractive to me, but there were some drawbacks as well. I was happy in my gymnastics show, and I didn't have a complete show of my own to perform. To perform a gymnastics show for fifty minutes as an individual was crazy. If I tumbled for the full fifty minutes, the audience would get bored and I would pass out. I knew I would have to develop a variety-type show, but the "variety" I should include was unclear. My guest entertainer friends made suggestions, and they encouraged me to start putting show ideas together. They then advised that if I ever had a chance to try some of my ideas for a short amount of time during a show, I should.

Eventually, the opportunity for me to experiment with some of my own show ideas came in the form of a farewell ship show. The farewell show is held the last night of the cruise, and three different entertainers who performed earlier in the week all come back to do around fifteen minutes each in a joint performance. One of our scheduled performers became sick and was unable to perform, so the cruise director asked if I could go out and perform for ten to fifteen minutes. It was the perfect opportunity for me! I could try out my show material, and since I felt like I was doing a favor for the ship, there was no pressure on me to be sensational.

Of the three entertainers who went on for the farewell show, I was the first to perform. Many of my comedian friends had given me several ideas of jokes and skills that they thought would be entertaining based on what they had seen me do, so I took a little comfort in that. I had been on stage my whole life, but the truth is, that night, I was very nervous about going on stage. I was doing something brand new for me, and I felt like I was not prepared for it at all.

I walked out on stage wearing a microphone headset. This allowed me to have both hands free to do my gymnastics and to speak at the same time. After introducing myself, I told the audience I wanted to try something different on this night. They had all seen me in the gymnastics show earlier in the week, and that helped me to believe that the crowd kind of knew me already and hopefully liked what they had seen. I explained that this time, I was going to do a silks routine for them. But, rather than just perform, I wanted to talk through the routine and tell them what I was thinking, tell them what the names of the tricks were, and give them insight into what it is like to be an Olympic gymnast. I climbed the silks and began my routine. I did one skill after another, and as I moved along, I joked about the positions I was in or I provided the audience with some history about how certain skills were invented. Some things they found funny. Some things they found interesting. Some things they must have found nothing in at all, for there was no response. That was a little unsettling, but I just continued doing my thing. It was a first for me, and everything I was doing was trial and error. The whole event was very raw, unrehearsed, and spontaneous.

After ten minutes of silks skills, gymnastics stories, and self-referencing jokes about what I was doing, I dismounted the silks to a rather surprising ovation. Although my act was completely unpolished and all new, the crowd seemed to really enjoy what I did. I concluded my portion of the show to that strong applause, and the cruise director was waiting for me backstage. He was very happy with what he saw me do, and he wanted me to do it again the following week. I saw this as a great situation for me to try out new material and to develop my own show, so I happily agreed to do it.

For the next six months, anytime I was on a ship, the cruise director would ask if I wanted to do my own short show segment. I happily experimented with different routines and material each week. I even started doing a little piano in the show, along with some singing. From the first day that I added singing, crowds seemed to like the change of tempo when I went to the piano, possibly because it was so unexpected. With the success of the singing, I threw in some juggling. It really caught on! I tried new things all the time, and if it was well received, I kept it in. If it was not well liked, it was out. This was the perfect way for me to choose and establish the material for my own developing variety show.

Eventually, after much encouragement from my guest entertainer friends, I was ready to formally launch the "Lance Ringnald Show" on ships. I created a video demo of what I had to offer, and one of my comedian friends offered to send it to his agent to see what he thought. After about three weeks, the agent called me and said he had seen my video and thought he could help me get some bookings. The fact that I was a former Olympic gymnast was a good selling point, but that only got me in the door. Once I was on the stage, either people would like my show and I would continue to work, or they would not like my show and I would be out of luck. I told my newfound agent that I would keep my second half of the year open for the possibility of getting bookings. This gave me about three months to finish doing my gymnastics production show on Norwegian Cruise Lines, and it gave me more time to plan for my future act.

About four weeks after I talked with my agent, he called me with some offers from Royal Caribbean Cruise Lines (RCCL). One offer was for a five-month contract. He said I didn't have to take the whole five months, and I could take a six-week break in the middle, but I thought I would just jump in, do the long contract, and see if it was going to work for me as a guest entertainer. My agent also mentioned that the offer was much better than normal initial offerings, which really indicated that Royal Caribbean liked what they saw on my video. It also happened to be 2004, an Olympic year, and my history as an Olympian may have influenced the offer of a long contract. Whatever the reason, my income more than doubled and I would be doing my own show, so I felt incredibly good about the offer.

I finished my final gymnastics production show on Norwegian, and even though I knew I would miss all the great people I had met and worked with there, I was also very excited about moving up and doing my own show. After a few weeks at home, RCCL flew me to Florida where I met my first RCCL ship. Right when I got on the ship, I learned that one of the other entertainers had missed his flight so I would be doing my show that very night—my first night aboard. My show was supposed to be twenty or twenty-five minutes long, and I was very prepared for that. However, because I was stepping in for someone else, I learned that I would also need to do another, different twenty-five minute show on the last night of the cruise. The first show was no problem; I felt like I had a very strong twenty-five to thirty minute show. But, to do a whole different show at cruise end was something I was not expecting to do. I didn't panic; I just realized I would have to think about that after the first show was over.

As hectic as it was to perform on my first night on the ship, I did not have time to think or to get nervous about anything, which was good. I went to the theater, rigged all my equipment, and got ready for the show that night. I met the stage staff and cruise director, and they were all very personable and helpful. After getting something to eat in the buffet, it was show time. I did my show twice that night, once for the first seating passengers and again for the second seating passengers. Both shows went really well, and both audiences seemed to be very entertained. I felt great. After the show, the cruise director told me that he had received several good comments about my show, and that also made me feel great. I was just so very content, because I felt that I had arrived at the next stage of my life and successfully reached another goal—doing my own show. After I realized the show was a success, I remember saying to myself, half-jokingly, "At least they won't fire me now!"

Though I had come in very confident about my show and what I could do, I had had no experience on any cruise line except NCL, so I had no way of knowing how well the show would go over on RCCL. I was grateful that my premier went so well. But, I couldn't quite relax. I still had to do another show at the end of the week, and it had to be different from the first one. So, I started putting ideas together. I had tried many different routines when I was on Norwegian, so I had the material. I just had to put it all together in a way that would make up an entertaining, well-designed show. By the end of the week, I had put together a different group of skills that would combine to make a show that I thought was good. I guess I made the right choices, because my second show also went over very well. I knew then that I was going to have a great time there for the next five months.

On most of the cruises, I only performed once in the week, doing my twenty-five to thirty minute show the last night of the cruise. I figured I had one hour of good material and routines, and I did not care how they split it up. The cruise director liked the fact that I was flexible with my different shows because if an emergency would arise and they needed someone to do a show at the last minute, I could do that.

Over the next five months of that RCCL contract, I practiced more juggling and silks, learned more songs on piano, and enjoyed sailing around the Caribbean while doing my show. It was a great contract, and like so many things we do for the first time, it was an experience I will always remember.

Passengers often seem to be surprised at how I have made the transition from the serious world of Olympic gymnastics competitor to the fun and more relaxed world of entertainment. That really flatters me that they recognize the transition, and I appreciate the interest in what it took to make the change. It truly was a difficult transition and one that could only be done over a very long period of time. Though I didn't expect it to happen, as time went by, I came to embrace the environment of entertainment even more than I had embraced the world of world-class gymnastics competition. Entertainment just seems to fit my personality very well, and it brings me closer to people as I give them insight into the world of gymnastics. I missed out on that human factor—that interaction—when I was in the intense world of competition.

Speaking of that human factor, the major difference between doing my old production gymnastics show with the group of singers and dancers and doing my own show is that now, I get to have that interaction with the audience that I enjoy so much. Every audience is different, so every show is different, and that is why I never get tired of doing my show. I still do my own show today, and I still love performing. I will continue to do this great job for as long as I can.

And now, as a veteran in entertainment, I can set my contract length the way I want it. Sometimes, I will do only one week on a ship before heading home again. It is nice, because I really like to be at home. The only problem, though, is that with shorter contracts, I have to travel more than I like. There is a lot of back and forth. So, when I get tired of the airports and travel, I might choose to do a longer contract, maybe up to six-weeks long, so I can settle on the ship for awhile. The freedom to set my schedule is something I did not have when I did my production show. I love that freedom now. I love working, but I also love being home where I can train, visit family, spend time in my own house, and teach gymnastics.

When I take a moment to look at my life, I can sincerely say that I feel very fortunate, because I have had so many incredible experiences and amazing highlights in the past. And now, not only do I get to travel around the world and see many great cultures and countries, I get to do the things I love to do, and I can also adjust the balance of time I spend on a ship and the time I spend on land. Yes, fortunate is a good word to describe how I feel.

Chapter 16

FREQUENTLY ASKED QUESTIONS

D uring my competitive years and even now, there are lots of questions that come from the media, from other athletes, and from regular people. Though I answered a lot of these in my life story, I will try to answer them specifically, and perhaps redundantly, here. Here goes.

HOW DOES IT FEEL TO BE AN OLYMPIAN?

I can't really put into words how it feels to be an Olympian, other than to say that it is indescribable. I'm surprised at how having the title of "Olympian" has stuck with me throughout my adulthood, and how much that title is recognized and respected. When people learn about my Olympic status, it tells them a lot about me, and it brings a lot of joy to me that they know what I have accomplished. It is like a gift that keeps on giving, in a way, because whenever I think about being an Olympian, even to this day, I am still extremely proud of that achievement. Of course, if I had never become an Olympian, I would not know what I was missing, and I would still focus on the highlights of my career. But, because I did become an Olympian, I have a unique perspective, and I love living with the fact that I have a respected and elite title attached to my gymnastics career. I will always be an Olympian, and that makes me feel special even now.

I would imagine that all Olympians think a lot about what the "title" means. I once heard Olympian Bart Conner asked by an interviewer how important being an Olympian was to him. He responded by saying something along these lines: "I love being an Olympian. I love everything that goes with being an Olympian. But if I had trained for the sixteen years that I did and not made it to the Olympics, do you think I would call that a failure? Of course not! That sixteen years of training, competing, learning, growing, and living was my success. I understand how the world respects and views Olympic athletes. Becoming one was the icing on the cake to an already very successful and full gymnastics career."

His answer does put things into perspective. He's commenting on reality, really, and I whole-heartedly agree with him. As athletes, we have to enjoy and embrace the process, or it is worth very little. It is the journey in which we should find the most value. Gymnastics is my passion, and when I was growing up, I was not that concerned about the Olympics. I was excited about that next skill I would learn, and I truly held on to the passion to work for it. Once again, nobody makes an Olympic team if they are not passionate about what they are doing. However, only a very small number of gymnasts will make the team every four years. There are a lot of gymnasts out there who are talented enough to make an Olympic team, but they are denied that dream for any number of reasons. They might have a bad competition, they might fall victim to injury, or they might lose their focus at the wrong time and experience a freak mental lapse. This is true of most all of the sports. Therefore, athletes should live in the day. If they love doing what they are doing day to day, with all the ups and downs, the future will take care of itself. There is success ahead, whether it involves being on the Olympic team or not. I was lucky, but I would consider myself lucky even if I had never made it to the Olympics. I loved my sport.

With that in mind, parents need to support, not push their kids in what they do. Encourage them and praise them when they earn it, and criticize and help them when they need it. Make the words constructive, and help kids to enjoy every minute of whatever they choose to pursue. And always, try to keep things balanced.

WHAT WAS THE HIGHEST POINT IN MY GYMNASTICS CAREER?

This question is difficult for me to answer because I was fortunate to have a few really amazing experiences in my career. But, when I really think about it, I would have to choose three different highlights that meant a great deal to me. They are all detailed in my story, but I'll list them again here.

The first one was making the Olympic team at the age of eighteen in 1988. That year, everything just fell into place, and I peaked out perfectly.

My second highlight was becoming World Champion on the high bar and third in the world all-around at the Goodwill Games in 1990. This happened right before my injury in '91, and I was in the best shape of my life. I was truly at the height of my ability. This competition was held in the United States, and to hear the national anthem being played while standing on the gold medal podium, right in my home country, was indescribable.

Making my second Olympic team in 1992 was the third highlight. To come back from a major injury and to overcome so much adversity in a short time—just in time to make my second Olympic team—was incredibly fulfilling to me.

As I experienced each of these highlights, I remember thinking at the time that that was my proudest accomplishment. I remember the feeling, and I remember the thrill. Nothing could have topped those moments. But now, when I look back, I view my entire gymnastics career as a highlight of my life.

WHAT IS THE TRUTH ABOUT PRESSURE IN COMPETITION?

I get a lot of questions about this. Each gymnast is an individual and may react a little differently to the pressure of competition.

However, the female gymnasts are typically very young and impressionable. This pressure can be more difficult for them to handle than it is for the older male gymnasts. This is not to say that the men don't also have difficulties dealing with pressure; it depends on the person. Actually, too much pressure is part of the reason the gymnastics world has raised the age to compete in an Olympics to sixteen. Officials felt that too much pressure was being put on too young of an athlete. For the young and inexperienced athlete to be thrust into the international scene without being trained both mentally and physically can be extremely stressful, if not damaging. Additionally, with the strict monitoring of diet and intense training of some of the most difficult and risky skills in the world, the pressure can intensify.

Imagine training several hours each day, five to seven days a week, all year long. When gymnasts finally find themselves in competition raising their hand to the judge and getting the okay to begin their routine, that is the one and only chance at that routine that they get. One slip of the hand? One misplaced step? These things could mean the difference between qualifying for an Olympic team or not, or even getting a medal or not. All these factors contribute to the pressure in the sport.

All sports have pressure, and the higher the level of competition, or the higher the expectations, the higher the pressure. Gymnastics may be unique because of the age and demand that is put on the athletes to produce. Occasionally, I will see a media report that focuses too much on the pressure and the more negative side of the sport. I am afraid that this leaves an inaccurate impression with spectators. Balance is the key to a healthy career. Pressure is a two-edged sword. It is exciting and potent, but it is also stressful. If one can find balance with pressure, I believe pressure has the potential to make one excel. Once again, the challenge becomes finding that balance.

CAN COMPETITIVE GYMNASTS
HAVE A NORMAL SOCIAL LIFE?

It seems there is always a question about whether or not a highly competitive gymnast can have a normal social life. My social life was within the world of gymnastics, and it was very normal to me. My best friends to this day are the friends that I made in the world of gymnastics. These friendships were made stronger by the empathy we all shared in pursuing the same goals, and by understanding each other and what we were experiencing to reach our goals. I also had friends in school, to whom I was known as "that gymnast," but I was always closer to my gymnastics friends. Though I was always in the gym, I never felt alone, I always had support, and I always had someone with whom I could laugh or cry. Therefore, I don't view a social life in the gymnastics world as better or worse than that of a social life in the "regular" world. I just view it as different.

WHAT DO GYMNASTS DO AFTER THEIR
COMPETITIVE CAREER ENDS?

For highly competitive gymnasts, that competitive life is intense. Once it ends, there is a strange, "What now?" feeling. Many former Olympic gymnasts will stay in the sport either through coaching, judging, or opening their own gymnastics business. Others go on to have more "normal" jobs, away from the world of gymnastics. Occasionally, they will go into entertainment doing things such as <u>Cirque du Soleil</u> or other acrobatic shows. I do think there are more gymnasts than other athletes who later go into the world of entertainment because they spend the majority of their young lives developing such great skills, and they get used to the idea of performing those skills before a crowd. When they finish competing, entertainment and gymnastics shows are growing fields in which they can put their talents to use.

HOW DO WE FIND GOOD COACHES?

Because the athletes in gymnastics are young and impressionable, it is very important to find a coach who is balanced and healthy in preparing gymnasts both mentally and physically. Coaches are not unlike parents—there are good coaches, and there are not so good coaches. There are several gymnastics programs out there, and the strong majority of them are very good with experienced coaches, safe coaching techniques, and safe equipment. Being part of an established and experienced gymnastics program is very important. Finding the right one only takes a little bit of research. I believe a good coach is one who can get the highest level of accomplishment out of his athlete while keeping balance among health, pressure, and productivity.

AREN'T THERE A LOT OF INJURIES IN GYMNASTICS?

Injuries are part of most sports, and gymnastics is no different. Of course, officials and coaches work very hard to keep their athletes safe, and over the years, gymnastics equipment has become safer and more efficient. It is becoming more so all the time. Even so, accidents happen, and unfortunately, that fact cannot be avoided. But, along with making sure equipment is safe, there are many ways that injuries can be prevented. As I mentioned regarding my own injury, the body does need to be respected, and coaches and athletes need to develop the ability to recognize when to work harder, when to back off, and when to get things checked out by a health care professional.

Most things only become unhealthy when they fall out of balance, and there are lots of things to watch for when it comes to preventing injuries. Watching one's diet is important. If an athlete becomes obsessed and out of balance, he or she may not eat enough or stay healthy enough to meet the demands of the sport, and that can open the door to injury. Being aware of pain is also important. A major imbalance of pain in training can lead to injury. An athlete must listen to his or her body. Pain is the body's way of saying it is being worked hard—sometimes too hard. As pain grows worse or unnatural, an athlete must respect it and find a safe, healthy remedy. Flexibility is another key to avoiding injury, so gymnasts and all athletes should nurture and maintain their flexibility throughout their days of involvement in their sports, and really, throughout their lives. Finally, being aware of one's ability is important. Athletes must respect a sport, and they must equally respect their ability to achieve certain skills within that sport. That means a person with no training in gymnastics should not walk into a gym and attempt a triple back flip. Gymnastics is based on safe, smart progressions. Coaches and athletes should be educated enough within their sport to know what to shoot for and how to get there safely and efficiently. They need to be smart, not irresponsible. Once again, it comes down to balance.

HAVE I HAD ANY MAJOR INJURIES?

Besides spraining my ankle pretty badly a couple of times (I healed in six weeks both times), the only major injury I have sustained was the injury to my shoulder in 1991. As I discussed in chapter 8, I tore my pectoralis major tendon from my humerus bone at the 1991 World Championships. That was the only debilitating injury I have had, and repairing that was the only surgery I had to go through in my thirteen years of competitive gymnastics. It took me about six months to recover from that—to get back to almost normal. I strained or pulled the occasional muscle now and then, and there was chronic pain at times, but because I was very flexible, I was very strong, and I made responsible decisions, I was able to prevent other injuries.

WHAT IS MY MOST EMBARRASSING MOMENT?

It's still embarrassing to me, just to answer this question. But, here goes. In 1989, just after the World Championships and while I was still in Germany, I was invited to travel from Germany to Switzerland for another competition. The competition was created to honor one of the members of the FIG (Federation of International Gymnastics). The Worlds were over and I was very relaxed, and I thought it would be cool to see Switzerland again. I had been there earlier that year for a mixed pairs competition. For that, I was paired with National Champion and Olympian Kim Zmeskal, and we won! Many of my international friends were going to this competition in Switzerland also, and the competition would be much less pressure-filled than Worlds, so I decided to go.

When we got to Switzerland, we had a few days before the meet, so we trained for a couple of hours each day and then went sightseeing in the city. On competition day, I was surprised at how much media was covering the competition. I hadn't expected that. To me and to the other gymnasts, it seemed to be more of a fun competition, one that wasn't too important in the world rankings. For the FIG, however, it was very prestigious, and they really built it up. It was heavily advertised, and it was to be televised on Swiss TV. It was a very big deal. The entire committee of the FIG was present, along with all the "Who's Who" of the gymnastics world.

The arena was very small and intimate—maybe a thousand people there—and although the best gymnasts in the world were invited, there were only about twenty competitors. We only had to do four events each, so it was not an all-around competition. Actually, it was more like an exhibition, but we would be judged, and we would receive scores. We didn't mind, of course. It was always good to see how we stacked up against other gymnasts at this level.

Before the competition began, I was told that after the competition, each gymnast would display a skill of his choosing, one for which he is known or one that is unique. I thought that was cool, and I decided to do a floor skill I had created. It was a skill called Russian circles, normally done on the pommel horse. Doing them on the floor repeatedly was very original at that time. After I decided what skill I was going to do, my mind was right back on the competition, and it went very well. When I was finished competing, I guess I forgot about the exhibition portion of this event. I started to change out of my competition uniform. That is when I heard an announcement come over the loud speaker—an announcement that contained my name. The announcement was not given in English, and my name was the only thing I understood, but it instantly reminded me that we all had to do the original skill of our choice.

I was half naked at the time, but I quickly started to put my gymnastics clothes back on, hurrying to get back to the floor. Fortunately, they did all the announcements in three different languages, ending with English, so I had that time to get dressed again. Just as I finished getting dressed, the English introduction was completed. I jogged out to the center of the floor in the small arena and waved to a very enthusiastic crowd. What I did not realize is that when I had put my clothes back on so quickly, I had put my shorts on backwards and inside out. The tag of the shorts was sticking out and waving in front, just as I waved to the crowd. Unaware of this, I went on to do my skill and waved to the crowd as I finished (as did my shorts). They applauded enthusiastically (almost too enthusiastically).

As I came off the floor, a friend of mine calmly said, "Look down." Sure enough, my bigger-than-I-realized shorts tag was sticking out for all to see. It was then that I understood why the crowd may have been overly enthusiastic. Even worse, I learned that Swiss TV had captured this moment live and up close, so everyone watching in Switzerland could see. All I could do was to laugh at this. Even the "Who's Who" members settled in those very close, reserved, front seats seemed to chuckle at my unfortunate moment. It ended up making a good story later. Much later (like now).

AM I DOUBLE JOINTED?

I am not even entirely sure what this means, but I get this question more than one might think. No, as far as I know, I am not double jointed. I am very flexible, and I think people may view that as being double jointed.

WHAT IS THE TRUTH ABOUT DRUGS IN SPORTS?

These days, it seems that performance-enhancing drugs are a bigger issue than ever before. I get a lot of questions about the use of steroids and enhancing drugs in the sport of gymnastics. In gymnastics, it is much better to be smaller and strong for one's own body weight. If a gymnast were to take steroids, not only would it do damage to the organs, it would also result in too much muscle bulk. To be a productive gymnast, athletes need to stay light, lean, and fast, and steroids are counterproductive to that. Also, enhancement drugs would tighten up the muscles and thereby take away one of the most important traits of a gymnast: flexibility. When a gymnast loses flexibility and becomes tighter, the muscles tear and strain much more easily, and injury becomes much more likely. Also, flexibility adds to the beauty of the sport and this helps gymnasts perform skills they could not do if they were not flexible. Drugs are simply unproductive and unhealthy.

I personally have never known any gymnast who was taking steroids or enhancement drugs while competing. The bottom line is that drugs are just detrimental to our sport—they are detrimental to life! Drugs rarely come up as a topic in gymnastics, and that is a testament to the health and cleanliness of the sport. Vitamins and a good diet are the best ways a gymnast can sustain the characteristics that make him or her healthy and great. That is common knowledge to gymnasts, and I think that is why we maintain a very clean sport.

Many people realize that there is a long list of banned substances in professional sports such as baseball, football, and others. What they may not realize is that for amateur sports such as gymnastics, or any Olympic sport, the list for banned substances is significantly longer than it is for professional sports. Certain cold medicines and other over-the-counter medicines may even be on the banned list, so gymnasts have to check carefully before taking any medicine at all. Caffeine is actually a banned substance, but the amount to test positive is the equivalent of about eight cups of coffee every two hours. That would be insane.

Though the list is long, it does help to keep all Olympic sports clean. While I was competing, there were often drug tests after a meet for several of the top finishers. It is something we accepted, and abusers were rarely found. In one tragic case, 2000 Olympic gymnast and all-around gold medalist Andreea Raducan of Romania actually had to forfeit her all-around gold medal shortly after her victory because she tested positive for pseudoephedrine, an over-the-counter medication. It was not a performance-enhancing drug, and no one claimed that it was. Even so, it was on the banned drug list. Raducan did not know that, and she only took it because her team doctor recommended it to help alleviate her cold symptoms on the day of her Olympic competition. Her teammate also took it, but she weighed more than Raducan, and she did not test positive. It was a horrible situation—heart-breaking, really—and it just goes to show that amateur athletes have to be very careful about what medications they use.

WHERE DO I KEEP MY MEDALS?

My medals from my most prestigious meets such as the Goodwill Games (world champion medals) and other international competitions, I keep in a safe place back home. I take them to speaking engagements with me sometimes because people seem to like to see them, and I am proud to show them. But, even though the medals are great, I take greater pride in what they symbolize— being the best or at the top in an event or in the all-around in the world of gymnastics. That is what gymnasts work so hard for and dream of. The medals symbolize that to me.

HOW LONG DOES A GYMNAST TRAIN FOR COMPETITION?

Every gym program is slightly different, and naturally, the level of a gymnast will determine the level of training. For me, when I made the Olympic team, we trained for three hours in the morning and three hours in the afternoon. We stayed on that schedule for three or four weeks before the Olympics. We would start off our workouts with a stretch routine that lasted around twenty minutes. Then, we would get to work training on the first three events, which were floor exercise, pommel horse, and rings. The other three events, vault, parallel bars, and high bar, would wait for the afternoon. We would do our routines over and over, and if we had any weak spots or problems, we would work hard to problem solve and fine-tune those skills. Many times, our coach would require us to hit three routines in a row with no major mistakes. If we had a major mistake, even on the third routine, we had to start all over until we hit all three routines perfectly, in a row. This helped us to become more consistent, and we definitely got stronger with our routines. It could also make for a very long training day if we were off a little that day.

After training our routines, we would finish with a short strength program. I did more strength in the off-season to get stronger, but when training for a major competition, we cut back on strength programs to concentrate and to be less tired to train routines.

Obviously this intensity of training cannot be maintained through an entire year, because it is too hard on the body. The more important the competition, the more intense the training for that competition. When I was not training for a major competition, a typical day of training may only last an hour and a half, or it might last up to four hours. It would just depend on what I needed to accomplish, or how well I achieved my goals. In the summers, when we were not in the competitive season, my workout length would really vary. When I was working new skills, I might spend more time in the gym because I wanted to learn them, and repetition, trial, and error were all important. Right before a meet, though, things were different. My pattern was to build up training before a major meet, then cut back, maintain, and rest the body a little between meets. Through the year I would adjust, trying to perfect and fine-tune my routines, making small changes when necessary, and adding difficulty as I learned new skills.

These days as a gymnastics entertainer, my training is much different. When I am on a cruise ship, I train around thirty to forty-five minutes a day, five days a week. It might not seem that long, but the strength I do is very gymnastics oriented and demanding. A non-gymnast would not be able to do much of it. I call this level of exercise "maintenance strength." It keeps me pretty strong, and it helps me to stay healthy and to avoid injury. When I am home and can go into the gym, I train around one and a half hours a day, five days a week, because I do more mainstream gymnastics skills as well as strength.

Anytime I work out, I start with a stretch program covering my splits, shoulders, back, and smaller joints to make sure I am warmed up properly. Whether a person is an athlete or not, I believe flexibility is a major key in staying free from injury, maintaining agility, and staying healthy. I also believe that consistency is the most important part of getting into and staying in shape. I know many people who go into a gym and work very hard, but in a week they are burned out and stop going. I believe it is much more productive for people to work out much less intensely but always consistently. Then, they can build up to greater intensity over time. People should make their workouts as challenging as they can but not so uncomfortable that they dread working out the next day.

HOW DO I STAY IN SHAPE NOW?

The downside to having such a high physical skill level and to making a living with it is that it is difficult to maintain as the body gets older. As I have mentioned before, I have found that consistency is the most important thing in the maintenance or development of anything. So, as I have gotten older, I have been very consistent with my training. Quality has overtaken quantity, and I train much smarter now.

Flexibility is a major factor in maintaining the body, and I have consistently maintained my flexibility and strength. Again, I do what I call "maintenance strength." This strength takes only about thirty to forty-five minutes a day, and I do it five days a week. Sometimes I will do more, but to maintain a healthy shape and to avoid injury, I feel that that amount of time works well for me. The strength I do is only slightly challenging for me. I don't make it so hard that I dread doing it the next day. As I have said, I don't believe anyone should ever work so hard in a workout that they dread the next one. Again, it is all about balance. Of course, a normal, non-gymnast could not do the maintenance strength I do, because my exercises are specifically gymnastics oriented. I do exercises such as handstand pushups and chest rollups to handstand, and other exercises that are unique to gymnastics students. It's calisthenics with a gymnastics twist, basically. I also wear a weight vest while doing these exercises. The vest I wear weighs ten pounds. It is all about maintaining the strength-to-weight ratio, and the vest really helps with that. When I work on a ship, it is more difficult to stay in shape because I don't have the gymnastics equipment I am used to working with. When I am home and not on a ship, I train much harder and always get into better shape because I am in a gymnastics gym. That's yet another reason I try to balance my time on a ship and my time at home. This balance has worked very well for me.

HOW LONG DO I STAY ON A
CRUISE SHIP WHEN PERFORMING?

This varies a lot, and it's changing all the time. But, on average, I spend around thirty weeks or more on different ships throughout the year. I will typically be on one ship for one to six weeks, and then I will take two weeks or so off between ship contracts. Each time I go to a ship, it is a separate contract for me. I now do different cruise lines, such as Royal Caribbean and Holland America, but I find myself on Royal most of the time. Even within the same cruise line, I perform on many different ships during the year. Some ships are incredibly large with huge theatres, and some ships are smaller with more intimate theatres. I enjoy each atmosphere that the different size ships and theatres have. When I get tired of traveling back and forth, I prefer to stay on one ship a little longer. When I want to be home more often, I will stay for shorter contracts.

When I am on land, I train at the gym where I trained for both of my Olympics. My coach is still there, and it's always good to see him. I also help coach when I am in the gym, and I really enjoy that. My passion remains very much in the world of gymnastics, so eventually, after I decide to cut back or stop entertaining, I will most likely coach.

I enjoy the cruise ships contracts, and I really do like being an entertainer, mostly because of the people who make up the audiences. However, I imagine that I cannot do this forever (I don't think so, anyway. Come see me when I'm eighty). Basically, as an entertainer on cruise ships, I get to do what I love to do, and I get to share other people's vacations—all while getting paid for it!

WHATEVER HAPPENED TO "GYM KIDS"—THE MOBILE GYM?

My friend Stacey ran Gym Kids, my mobile gymnastics club, for me when I first started working on the cruise ships. She actually ran it for several years while I cruised, and I really enjoyed "visiting" Gym Kids whenever I was home. But, eventually, I realized that my cruise ship job had, indeed, become a permanent thing. Likewise, eventually, Stacey was ready to move on and coach full time at Gold Cup, the gym in which I had trained for my two Olympics. So, in 1997, we closed the business and sold the gymnastics equipment to Burch, Gold Cup's owner and head coach. It was sad to see Gym Kids go, but I still look back fondly at what it became. There are still former Gym Kids running around out there, and many of them are involved in gymnastics to this day.

Chapter 17

OPINIONS AND INSIGHTS

After over a decade of competition, training, failure, success, and reflection, I have developed many thoughts about what has helped me to achieve what I wanted to achieve, and about what has helped to bring me happiness and peace over the years. That they are included here should be no surprise; as I have mentioned throughout my story, I am a pretty pensive, philosophical, and analytical guy. I think that thinking about life, sports, goals, and dreams only adds to them, because it helps to make sense out of why people do the things they do, and it paves a way for us to all get through life with more understanding and empathy for each other. The result of that can only be for people to be a little bit happier, right? It makes me happier, that I know. I know that my experiences have only been enhanced by my thoughts about them, whether before, during, or after the events, and even though my competitive gymnastics career has come to an end, I still feel very strongly about the philosophies I developed during my career. These next sections are simply a few final expressions of my appreciation of some of the best things in life, and of the philosophies that have become a part of me.

The Best Things in Life

PEOPLE'S PERCEPTION OF AN OLYMPIAN, AND OF OTHERS

When I became an Olympian, my perspective was much different from that of the people around me. I was always looking at the gymnasts I admired, hoping to learn from them and to get better. While training, I was very critical of myself, and I tended to concentrate most on the areas where I was weak—the areas where I knew I had to improve in order to move up in the world of gymnastics.

It has occurred to me that when people see Olympians, they don't seem to see any of those weaknesses, and they generally offer unsolicited attention and respect. This took me a while to get used to. That instant respect was always a surprise to me, but it taught me a lot.

To this day, I think one of the most wonderful things people can have happen to them is to be able to do something they love to do for as long as they can do it, and then to have many other people recognize and respect them for doing it. I have been lucky enough to feel that for much of my life. It became even more potent on the cruise ships, because even though they are like small "cities," ships are also very confined spaces, and we work around the same people everyday. They instantly respected my gift, and I soon began to realize that I needed to look for theirs. We all need to look for people's gifts, we need to develop an understanding of what it is they pour their lives into, and we need to respect them for what they do.

INDUCTION INTO THE UNITED STATES GYMNASTICS HALL OF FAME

In 2000, I was inducted into the United States Gymnastics Hall of Fame. This is one of the highest honors anyone can obtain in our country in the sport of gymnastics. The ceremony took place at the National Championships Banquet in Philadelphia. Once again, to be honored at such a high level for something I truly loved was incredibly fulfilling. Also, to be invited into a select group of truly gifted gymnasts was wonderful. To become a recognized part of gymnastics history in this country was both amazing and humbling. There is no higher honor for me than to be forever recognized for contributions and accomplishments within my sport. In my acceptance speech, I found it very difficult to think of all the people who had contributed their knowledge and skills to help me obtain my life long goals. There were people whom I had met in my career just in passing that with just one word or phrase had a major impact on me. Of course my coach, family, and fellow competitors and teammates had the most direct impact, but there were many other people who were a part of my success. Just as when I became an Olympic gymnast, being honored for my accomplishments brought a euphoria I would have never imagined possible. It is something I will never forget.

TRYING TO BE UNIQUE IN THE SPORT

One of my friends from the 1984 U.S. Olympic gold medal team once told me that each generation of athletes stands on the shoulders of giants. I believe that what he meant was that when a person creates something original or does something for the first time, he becomes the leader, and everybody else will try to emulate him. Of course, I view this through the eyes of a gymnast. I see that in successive generations of gymnasts, the athletes will view those who have gone before them with respect and admiration. They—the next generation of gymnasts—begin their careers, they see and learn what the previous generation created, and they build on to that previous originality. They try to create and perfect new skills and trends, pushing the level of difficulty even higher. That makes what all of us do during "our time" all the more important. If gymnasts are innovative and creative within their discipline, their contributions will be felt for generations to come. I always loved this dynamic of the sport, one with such a powerful cause and effect. When athletes compete at the world-class level, it is very difficult for them to be unique and to come up with original skills or combinations, because everyone is so good. I was very proud to come up with a few skills and combinations that contributed to the advancement of the sport of gymnastics. For example, I was the first gymnast in the U.S. to perform three major release moves in a row on the high bar. The skills were a *reverse hecht*, another *reverse hecht*, and a *Gienger*. It was a very difficult sequence because I had to catch each release move at an almost perfect distance from the bar in order to perform the next release immediately after. I made it work, and people even called me "The Release Man" for a while! This set a trend for the next generation of combinations of release moves in gymnastics. Although my goal was to be unique and better than the other athletes on the gymnastics events, to see other gymnasts start to work on this combination or on other skills I may have introduced or innovated was a true compliment.

There were other skills I was very proud of, as I was the athlete who did them for the first time. I did a trick called a *Maltese* on the parallel bars; I did a skill called a *Stutz* to one rail, or what is called an English handstand on the parallel bars; I did a back flip off the pommel horse; and I did a one and a half twisting one and three quarter flip to roll out in the laid out position on floor. This had been done tucked, but never in the layout position before. These skills that I did for the first time, or the ones to which I added my own characteristics, ultimately helped me become an Olympic gymnast but also contributed to the world of gymnastics. I can see now what they have led to in the generations to follow, and it's a great feeling. I think we all like to see people following in our footsteps, and it's a true testament to those who have gone before when the next generation works extra hard to surpass the accomplishments of their heroes. I take tremendous joy and pride to have made any contributions, and I am humbled to see that my accomplishments have motivated the generations to come.

MORE ON INNOVATION

A lot of people have asked me how Olympians set themselves above the rest. That's a good question, and though I can't claim to have the ultimate answer to it, my thoughts on it apply to gymnastics as well as to anything where people are in competition, which stretches to many areas of life. Basically, setting ourselves above the rest means we need to do what everybody else is doing, and then we need to do it better. That's pretty conventional, but there is more to it. I believe that if people want to reach the top and stay there, they have to be original. They have to be innovative.

So, how do we come up with original things, or innovation? It takes a lot of work; it also takes a lot of mistakes. There are a lot of glamorous things about being an Olympian. The physical nature of the sport keeps us in shape, we get to travel, and the title of "Olympian" is generally respected. But, the process of becoming an Olympian is not very glamorous at all. Speaking on behalf of the Olympic gymnasts, we are constantly in the gym, falling as we try to make the most difficult skills in the world look as easy as possible. What people see on TV is the best the athletes can offer, following a lifetime of mistakes. Yes, we are all taught to learn from our mistakes, and we often do. And, for gymnasts, sometimes it is those mistakes that lead to originality. For example, there was once a gymnast who was working on a skill called circles. For gymnasts to do circles, they need to keep their legs tightly together and then swing their legs around in an aerial-view circle, all the while supporting themselves on their hands and shifting their weight from hand to hand each time their legs go by. Sounds simple, right? Anyway, this gymnast could circle pretty well, but no matter how hard he tried, he just could not keep his legs together. That is a big deduction in gymnastics. Another gymnast who was watching saw this mistake and thought that if that gymnast could not keep his legs together, he should try straddling them—keeping them very far apart through the entire circle. The gymnast who was watching decided to try it. His name was Kurt Thomas, and eventually this skill turned into what is now called the *Thomas Flair*. What came from a mistake became an innovative skill, and it revolutionized gymnastics on the pommel horse.

This just goes to show that mistakes can open the boundaries of imagination. They open the mind to ideas that might never surface if we did everything right the first time we tried.

ADJUSTING TO LIFE AFTER GYMNASTICS

It is a major adjustment to go from training everyday to living a "normal life." As a competitive gymnast, I was challenging myself, I was competing all around the world while representing my country, and I was being recognized and acknowledged for that almost everywhere I went. It was what fed me, and it kept me going. When retirement came, things naturally changed.

Some gymnasts enter instant retirement. I believe that is the hardest way to go, for to suddenly stop and to no longer get any nourishment from the food that has sustained them all that time would, of course, be a shock to the system. I was lucky, because I gradually fell out of competition and into gymnastics entertainment and coaching, so that still allowed me to be partially a gymnast. My transition was very smooth. But, even with my subtle change from world-class competition to teaching and performing, I noticed a void—a hunger—for what I had had before. Of course that is natural to a degree, but it can be very traumatic to some. For many other gymnasts and athletes, the transition is not so gradual, so it is much more traumatic. It is difficult for athletes to spend all their life developing skills and abilities only to reach a day when they don't need those skills anymore, or when those needs no longer serve them or their purposes.

Due to physical or mental demands, very few sports allow anyone to stay at the top of their game for very long. Thus, to stay sane, the gymnast/athlete must be prepared to re-invent himself or to find another avenue in which he can apply all his effort during that after-competition life. This is what most athletes have to deal with at one point or another. The higher the level and the longer the career, the more traumatic it is for the athlete when retirement finally comes. It is kind of like a Hollywood child star that has so much attention in his youth that when he grows up, if he gets out of the business, he has an identity crisis. It's all about the "What do I do now?" question.

This is a tricky thing. I believe that faith, family, and friends are the primary ways we can find strength through these transitions. After that, when a major change comes, the main thing, I believe, is to find something else to bring on a challenge and to have goals to reach for. It's vital to find passion for something else to grow in, to feel cause and effect as well as purpose in life. Giving back to others is one way to make this happen, because we need to learn, eventually, that it's not all about us. It has been for our whole lives, but in order for us to find peace, we have to look beyond ourselves. Athletes are used to focusing, used to putting lots of energy toward a goal. I feel that they can get past the grief of saying goodbye to a sport if they can learn to focus on something new, on something else, using the mental skills they learned in their sport in whatever they pursue afterwards. These skills may seem secondary at first, but the attitude, the mental experience, and the clear thinking under pressure will help them to succeed at pretty much anything.

I believe that one characteristic I possess that helped me to become an Olympic gymnast and to excel in the sport was what I call "obsessive passion." I referred to it often in my story. I realized early on that once I found that I like doing or learning something, I would become obsessed with it. Because it became my passion, it was not work to me anymore; it was fun, and I could do it end-lessly. This is why I still believe that no matter what people do, if they can make it fun, they will learn it much faster and much more efficiently. The benefit of my own obsessive passion was that I learned and became very proficient in whatever I became passion-ate about. The downside is that my passion would often take over, and everything else in my life would take a back seat. I believe this imbalance is present in many successful athletes, and though it can be very productive for excelling at something, it is yet another reason why it is so difficult for high-level athletes to move on once their "sport" comes to an end. My solution has been to use that obsessive passion to pursue new challenges, and then to use what I have learned to somehow serve others. That's where that essential balance enters in. We can still focus, we can still challenge our-selves, and then we can give back to the world that has served us for so long. In doing so, we'll be nourished and satisfied once again.

Philosophies

COACHING

I believe a <u>good</u> coach is someone who is able to motivate his athletes to do the work necessary to succeed. I believe a <u>great</u> coach is someone who is able to motivate his athletes to WANT to do the work necessary to succeed. People learn more efficiently when they are having fun learning, and when the motivation is internal. Of course, this is often easier said than done. But, making the sport in which an athlete wants to excel a fun thing should be a goal and an essential part of the training. That is not to say it won't still be hard work. Hard work goes with the territory. But, the work should be rewarding, and it should bring satisfaction to the athletes.

With that said, it is very important for individuals to know how they learn best. Some learn visually, so when they see a trick, they understand it well and can begin the learning process. Others learn much better through explanations, so they need much more than just a demonstration to know how to proceed. It's the basic visual versus oral learning idea. I am a visual learner, so when I see something, I usually understand it very easily. That is precisely why I used to watch gymnastics videos endlessly—to enhance my own learning. I knew that if I had to depend on someone just explaining things to me, I might not understand very quickly, or at all. It's imperative for coaches to get to know their athletes, so they will know what their athletes need to learn and how to teach them most efficiently.

No matter how I felt about the many coaches I had throughout my career, I can see that all of them had something to offer me in reaching my goals. Everybody has some personal characteristics about them that others may not like, but it is important to not let that block out the positive things someone has to offer. This holds true with coaches, but I believe it also holds true with people in general.

I have said before that being the best in the world at a sport does not make someone the best person in the world. It just makes him or her the best athlete. Being a good person and being a good athlete are two different things, and I feel many athletes and many non-athletes do not recognize this fact. Respect for being a good athlete can be demanded from an athlete. Respect for being a good person can only be offered by another. Coaches who know how to instill this in their athletes are a step above the rest.

PREPARATION

It was John Greenleaf Whittier who said, "Of all sad words of tongue or pen, the saddest are these: 'It might have been.'" I agree with that concept, and throughout my life, I have done all I can do to avoid those saddest of words. I recognized early on that every minute of preparation counts. Thus, when it comes to shooting for a goal, I believe people should do everything in their emotional, moral, and physical power to prepare the best that they can. If they do that, no matter what the outcome, they will have a strong peace in knowing they did all they could. They will never ask themselves that horrible question, "What if I had done more?"

As a gymnast, I could have easily thought things like that, telling myself that if I had just done one more routine or spent one more hour on strength, I would have been more successful. I knew many gymnasts who would get to a competition and wish they had had a little more time to prepare. That is probably natural, but I did not have that feeling. When I got to a competition, I normally felt that I had done all I could do to prepare the best that I could, and even if I had the chance to go back in the gym for another month, it would not have made me any better than I was. That is what everyone should shoot for. That is when people know they have prepared well.

In order to achieve that complete preparation, I always did enough to make sure I had no room for regrets, or for a desire for "more time." I determined early on that I would not leave one event to go train on the next event if I did not feel good about my training. I also developed my own personal standards I had to live up to, and I learned to evaluate myself productively on a bad day more often than on a good day. We are all good on a good day. How we are on a bad day defines our character. On a bad day of training, I learned how strong or weak my weakest link was in my chain of gymnastics. If I could hit all my routines when I was feeling weak or bad, that gave me confidence no matter how I felt in a competition because I knew I could do it. Throughout my career, I never held back. I trained hard, I trained productively, and I never looked back to say, "What if. . .?"

Considering that preparation, I think there are many ways people can mentally prepare for something, and not everybody does it the same way. I remember that before some competitions, I would worry and stress out a lot. With other competitions, I did not worry nearly as much. To this day, I cannot say why I would get more nervous before one meet over another. But, it seems that the more nervous I got before a major competition, the more relaxed I was during the actual thing. That leads me to believe that my anticipation was a form of mental preparation. If I did not concentrate or anticipate a competition before hand, I would be surprisingly nervous during it because I had not gone through the process of my normal mental preparation.

There was a mental game I used to play at competitions, and it served me well. I see now that it can help in many situations in sports or otherwise. My ploy was to let my mind wander into the future, and face the very moment that I feared could happen. Maybe I feared a fall, a bobble, or a brain lapse. I would picture that moment, I would concentrate on how it felt, then I would come back into real time and realize that that moment had not happened yet. I would then tell myself that I had the power to change the future. I could be proactive and fix the problem before it occurred, so I would never have to face that event and I could avoid that feeling of failure. Right before I mounted an event, especially if it was one about which I felt uneasy, I would fix the mistake in my mind, salute the judges, and perform to the best of my ability. I did this often in competition, and it worked wonders for me.

Mental games, mental preparation, no regrets—it all goes to show that it is very important for athletes to be strong, both mentally and physically. Physical health and mental health are very much a part of each other, and they develop over time. If people are mentally strong, then it is easier for them to get physically strong. Likewise, if people are physically strong, it is easier for them to get mentally strong. Naturally, this applies negatively wherever there is weakness. Athletes, especially at high levels, need to be fully aware of the connection between the two, so they will give both areas the attention they need and be better prepared for whatever comes.

LONGEVITY

It is very hard to reach the top in any sport. It is almost impossible to stay at the top. So, how do athletes stay at the top of their game or achieve longevity? First, when athletes start to work for a goal, any goal, things usually get worse before they get better. For example, let us consider flexibility. If athletes want to get more flexible, they begin to stretch. If the stretch is intense, the first day may be a little uncomfortable. Then, during the next day or two, the athletes will probably feel much worse and much tighter—not more flexible—because the muscles tighten up after stretching. Many people stop stretching when they hit the sore stage because it is unpleasant, but if they choose to work through the sore, more difficult stage, they will eventually become much more flexible and reap the benefits of hanging in there.

That idea isn't new, nor is it limited to sports. Maybe someone has a great idea to open a business and can't wait to get started. Then, he or she starts taking the steps to open that business and learns that there is much more to it than first thought. In the frustration of having to do more than anticipated, or of losing money for the first few years, new business owners might give up on opening that business all together. Or, they might be tempted to close it down when the going gets rough. But just think: if they could stick with it, there is a very good chance they could reap the benefits in the long run. Sure, there is the "unknown" to factor in, but the unknown could be a very good thing, and if people don't give that unknown a chance, they will never know.

Back to the athletic perspective: Maybe someone wants to get into better shape, so he or she starts going to the gym. After the first week, any newcomers to a gym are very sore, and more than likely, they have already grown to hate the gym. But, if they push through the pain, there can be great rewards afterwards. This dynamic happens all the time, and in many different ways. True change comes only through growth and time. Most ideas, dreams, or goals that we have are more difficult to reach than we think. But, it is in pushing through the difficult times that great things can come. To get through those difficult times, remember that how much people do in the gym or in a workout is not as crucial as the fact that they are consistent in going to the gym each day. People should not give so much of themselves in one day that they dread going back the next day. They should give all that they can, making sure to leave with enough to give the next day. If they give too much, they will stop giving all together. If they don't give enough, they will not grow or progress, and they will never reach their full potential. It's all about balance. And, balance leads to longevity.

Of course, whatever we choose to do for a long time can lead us right into the "burnout" trap. Burnout comes from a lack of that all-important balance. Balance will bring peace, and imbalance will bring stress. I admit that for a while, when I was competing, I had an imbalance of the passion and energy that I was applying to my gymnastics. The upside to that was that I excelled as a gymnast. The downside, though, is that I neglected some other things in my life. I began to realize that the brain, as well as the energy we use, is like a pie cut into several pieces. Some people may have a large piece of pie for math, so they are brilliant with numbers. Those people might have smaller pieces of pie for geography, so they might get lost easily. I think it's normal for everyone to have a bigger piece of pie in the area of their talent and passion, but we really need to take the time to taste some of those other pieces and to enjoy the variety they can add to our lives. If we don't, that imbalance on the side of giving far too much to one thing will lead to burnout and rob us of our peace and our longevity. When we have peace, we'll share the better part of our nature with the world, and the world will be a better place for it. Naturally, this should be our goal.

When the focus must be on that largest piece of pie, burnout will inevitably set in. I have found that the best thing an athlete can do in that case is to distract himself or herself with things that are productive, within or even outside of the sport. When I was burned out from doing my routines over and over again, my teammates and I started to play games in the gym. One of our favorites was "Add-on." For Add-on, I would do one trick, and then my teammate would do that same trick and add his own trick. The third person would do those first two tricks and then add his own third trick, and so on. As the game went on, we ended up working our tails off but really, for us, it was a game and a completely different mental approach to training. It helped us to get away from the same old routine without truly taking us away from training. Our goal was to win the game, not to work; the work was the side effect. The challenge brought out our best effort, as challenges often do for most people, but it also served as a fresh distraction. We loved the game, but we still trained well and accomplished something necessary and worthwhile.

In addition to making training fun, another thing that helped me to obtain longevity in gymnastics was making my daily workout or routine like morning coffee. Many people have coffee or tea in the morning to get them going, and they don't even think about it. It is a routine they go through each day, and eventually, it becomes a habit. That's how it was for me. For instance, when I was training, I loved handstand push-ups, but I hated presses. I got in the habit (I made it my morning coffee) of doing a press to get to a handstand to do my handstand push-ups, and eventually, I got better at presses. I even learned to like them. In the same way, I used to go into the gym and warm up a little, and before I even started my workout session, I would do some basic strength and balance sequences on the different apparatus. It only took about fifteen minutes, and it helped me to maintain my fundamentals. I did not think about it, and I did not dread it. In fact, I had very few feelings about it at all. It simply became like morning coffee—it became a habit, and it got me going. I did these little fundamental routines for my entire gymnastics career. It got to the point where I did not want to work out until I had done those little routines. And, the habit of working out has stayed with me. Though I no longer compete, I still work out every single day. I never dread it—it is just part of who I am.

A final thought on longevity. We have to keep things fun and exciting, or we will not even desire longevity. Consider this: as we get older, we get more set in our ways. We accept the most common or conventional ways of doing things. In other words, we start to live within conventional boundaries, or within a box. Sure, it might be comfortable there, but it can also be dull, and it can keep us from experiencing the joy of seeing something new. As children, we really have no box. The only kind of thinking we can do is outside the box, and each new day brings exciting, stimulating experiences. We see no reason why we cannot do something—there are no limitations, and no dream seems impossible. If we can find ways to do things as adults that will require the energy, imagination, and open-mindedness we had as children, and if we can mix that with the maturity and wisdom that we gain as we grow older, there is very little we cannot do. Enthusiasm, eagerness, good health, and longevity will come when we, as "responsible adults," hold on to that energy and imagination we had in our youth.

SETTING GOALS AND
DEVELOPING HEALTHY HABITS

One thing I have learned over time is that we can choose and develop our own habits—good ones and bad ones. Therefore, people need to be very aware of their choices. Habits tend to start off as conscious acts, but because of repetition and conditioning, they become unconscious motions or activities people don't even necessarily realize they are doing. They become automatic. And, because it is hard to hate or dread something of which people are hardly aware, most people don't often think to question their habits. They don't have deep feelings about them at all until they stop themselves and truly evaluate what they are doing. Of course, most people recognize that once they develop a habit, it is a part of them, and it is very hard to kick. If it's a bad habit, people should do all they can to kick it soon. If it's a good habit, great! Just imagine how a good habit can help push people toward their goals!

Let's say that a man wants to lose some weight and get into better shape. He decides to go to the gym. He starts to work out, and though he really hates it, he pushes himself hard and finishes the workout. The next day comes, and because the goals remain the same—to lose weight and get into shape—he returns to the gym and pushes himself very hard once again. Again, he hates it. He feels weak, and he wants to avoid his area of weakness. And, the process is not fun for him at all. He begins to reinforce his hatred for working out, and it gets worse each day. Eventually, he will hate it so much that he will stop going. To build a positive workout habit, this man needs to get rid of that feeling of hatred and dread before he goes to the gym. Otherwise, his efforts will never have a good result. It is more important for him to build a positive workout habit than to force himself to work through frustration and negative feelings.

So, what is the solution for him? He should keep going to the gym, but he should work out very lightly. He should not demand too much of himself, and while he's getting started, he should just try to do the things he enjoys at the gym. Making his workout fun will help to turn his weakness into strength. Then, he will not dread going back. Eventually, he will get into a rhythm, he will build momentum, he will try new things, and he will get stronger. His gym experience will become a positive habit rather than a negative, torturous event.

That approach really applies to many aspects of life. There might be a big picture in mind, but in order to achieve it, people should create several small goals to serve as stepping-stones to reach that ultimate goal. When people have a long-term goal, or a very intense goal, it is easy for them to lose motivation or to become overwhelmed when the goal is not easily met. They might get discouraged when they don't get to see immediate results and progress. With short-term goals, or stepping-stones, the results come more easily and more often, which gives people motivation to go on to the next step. It is often said that a thousand mile journey starts with just one step. That first step is the goal, and it is typically the hardest step to take. But once it is reached, the next step comes more easily. Soon, the journey of a thousand miles is well underway. And, each milestone brings satisfaction, fulfillment, and energy to go on. Each step brings more progress, more hope, and more fuel for a good habit.

Of course, as people develop healthy habits and reach toward their goals, it is important for them to have a healthy and true recognition of their strengths and weaknesses. Goals can be big, but they must be realistic, or the steps will lead to disappointment. But, big goals can lead to amazing journeys, and it is more possible than many people realize to use the resources all around them to make up for their weaknesses. The world is an amazing place, and dreams can come true. If they don't, though—if that dreaded "failure" comes along—it is not the end of the world.

When I was competing, I naturally had big goals. And, each competition served as a stepping-stone for what I needed to change, strengthen, or do to obtain the next goal. So, for me, having a bad competion felt like being knocked down to the floor. I'm sure "failure" is that way for many people. And, each time it happens, it is harder to get back up again. It is vital to have some success between the knock-downs so hope and motivation can stay alive, but sometimes that does not happen; no one can count on that. So, when I failed, I vowed I would never do it again, and my determination was a strong sense of motivation. But, sometimes I would forget that feeling, and the motivation that the fear of failure gave me would start to fade. I learned then that how I handled my failure could create my defining moments and my future growth. I realized that I needed to remember how strong I felt about the failure at the time so I would not repeat the same mistakes. I learned to have no fear of set backs. I decided to let them strengthen my resolve to overcome obstacles. My determination was driven by my passion, and it helped me to turn my dreams into reality. That, in turn, made success much sweeter.

With that said, people must remember to set realistic but big, exciting goals. The impossible is only impossible until someone does it, and maybe a "failure" today will drive them toward a huge success tomorrow. When people define what they want, they should be relentless. They should never waste their energy, so all their actions should be intentional. If they feel they are unstoppable, they will become so. And, no matter what the goals are, people need to enjoy the journey. They should try new things to keep life exciting, and they should make the most of their time. No one knows when they are young what the future holds. For gymnasts, no one can predict who will make an Olympic team. There is always the risk of injury, the body constantly changes, progress is unpredictable, and there is always the possibility of a loss of motivation. But, if an Olympic team is someone's dream, he or she should put everything into the efforts and enjoy the journey, wherever and no matter how far it goes. Then, there is success at the end no matter what.

Finally, remember that people are like houses, with several rooms inside. Just as we spend more time in some rooms than in others, we explore some parts of ourselves more than others. As people set goals and develop habits, they should look into those neglected rooms and explore a little bit. They might be surprised by what they find there.

THE CONCEPT OF "PASSION"

Just imagine what would happen if we could choose the areas in which we had talent, or about which we wanted to be passionate. What would we choose? As it is now, we are created with certain gifts and talents, and when we are passionate about something in which we have talent, the odds of us reaching high goals in that area are pretty good. Without both talent and passion in place, however, success is a battle, because though people can go far on talent, they need passion to reach the top. Nobody makes an Olympic team unless they have true passion for the sport in which they are gifted. The trick is to create passion for something in which we may have talent, but no desire to pursue. It is in that situation that we need to pool all our resources. For example, when I was young, I used to be afraid of the high bar, and I never wanted to train on it. I loved the pit, though, because nothing was more fun than flipping into a huge hole filled with foam blocks that would safely break my fall. My coach recognized my talent, and he also recognized my lack of passion for the high bar. So, he established the rule that I was only allowed to use the pit when I trained on high bar. Needless to say, my love for the pit overpowered my fear of the high bar, and I eventually developed a passion for high bar. I went on to become world champion on that very event. My coach helped me learn to take the passion I had for one thing and use it to positively affect something else.

Passion for something is a powerful source of motivation. But, passion is often accompanied by other powerful emotions and forces. As an Olympian, I have observed a lot of athletes. Over time, I have seen and concluded that athletes are typically driven to a goal by one of two things: opportunity or fear. In competition, some athletes had that eye-of-the-tiger attitude, and they saw each competition and pressure situation as an opportunity to show the best that they had, or to reach their goal. Others were driven by the fear of failure, and they did everything in their power to avoid that failure. It is important for people to recognize what motivates them. Fear and opportunity are diametrically opposed to one another as types of motivation, but they are both powerful tools. Personally, I was driven by the fear of failure so often that I would train, think, and prepare harder than a lot of my peers just to avoid that feeling of failure. When athletes know what drives them, they can work to find a balance, and their training can be enhanced.

If we truly know in what area our talents and passions lie, we need to pursue that area. Again, this comes down to balance because again, passion is very powerful. I believe that a man without passion is sort of like a tiny firecracker. There is not much to be gained or lost. But, a man pursuing his passion is like a nuclear bomb. There is a lot of power to be harnessed. If it gets out of balance or out of control, it can explode and do a lot of harm. But, if it is pursued with balance, it can provide an endless supply of energy. We should all be lucky enough to find that area that entices us, that thrills us, and that allows us to shine. Some people are fortunate enough to make a living with their passion. If that isn't possible, then I advise them (as I did in Chapter 5) to get a simple job or to find other means that will support them and at the same time allow them to pursue their gift on the side. We don't want these passions to fizzle out!

THOUGHTS ON PEOPLE

I believe there are only two ways for one person to interact with another person: productively, or unproductively. To interact with people productively, I think it's good to think about what makes people tick. Over time, I have decided that some people are like frisbees and some are like boomarangs; some people are like helicopters, and some are like airplanes. They all work a little differently, but they all fly. As we are all placed here to soar in the same skies, we should remember that it is not our job to try to change an airplane to a helicopter. Instead, we can try to learn from the airplane. It is in our diversity that we have a bigger knowledge pool. I say this from experience. The other athletes with whom I have trained have had different ways of learning, different techniques, and different styles. The same holds true for the coaches, the judges, and even the rules of the game. I recognize now that I was made better through our differences, and it was because of those differences that I learned to be who I am today.

As we consider people's differences, we must also acknowledge that everyone has the potential to do something incredible. But, it seems that for people to achieve something truly great, they need to have a challenge. Otherwise, they see no need to work for anything, and there is nothing to drive them. Whether it is in sports or in other areas of life, people naturally train to the level of their environment. They ease up if nothing pushes them, and they rise to meet challenges or expectations when they sense the need. I know that if gymnasts work out with other average gymnasts, it is easy and common to relax, and to be average gymnasts themselves. But, if gymnasts step into an environment where the other gymnasts are all very advanced, they tend to push themselves to keep up with the others, or to surpass them, so they naturally advance much faster.

This seems to be a common human characteristic. It is only the unique and great ones who do not train or perform based on the level of their environment. Those select few are self-motivated, and they push themselves to work at the highest level of their potential no matter when or with whom they work. They push their limits all the time, and they achieve true greatness. We should learn from those unique individuals. We could accomplish such amazing things if we would all train, work, and learn to our highest potential at all times, even in environments that do not provide that external stimulation.

No matter how much motivation we have and what we accomplish, we must never forget that we are flawed as humans. And, it seems that way too many people don't give themselves the freedom to be flawed. That does not mean they should justify their flaws, but they should release some of that pressure they put on themselves, and they should move past those imperfections. They should also recognize that life itself is flawed, and it is very unpredictable. If we drive in a car for a long journey, say one thousand miles, we prepare the car, not the road. We have to take the road as it comes. That is the picture of life. We are the car, and we need to take care of ourselves. If we are prepared properly, if we are healthy—physically and mentally—then we are tuned up and prepared for the journey of life, with all its ups and downs. When we are healthy, we can even handle the potholes in the road, and we can get back on the road if we ever hit a detour and feel lost or disjointed. We can always look forward to the road ahead. In the end, we can have peace in the completion of our one thousand mile journey.

EXTRA TIPS FOR GYMNASTICS. . .AND FOR LIFE

When I went to the Olympics, I had never wanted to win anything so badly in my whole life. The feeling of reaching a goal was intoxicating to me. I think that kind of drive sets the successful ones apart from the "other" ones. It's not really the outcome that is the significant factor. It shouldn't be, anyway. No matter what the truly great ones do or what level they achieve, they want to do their best, and they give it their all. That is where the success comes in. As a gymnast, it was in reaching for goals and doing all I could do that I found happiness. Because I have always gone for things honestly, morally, and ethically, there is never a goal that I have reached that has made me unhappy. I know that if I reached a goal in a way that was not moral or honorable, I would not have been happy. People should analyze their approaches and their efforts, and to reach true success, they should always maintain honorable standards.

If challenges creep up—and they will—remember that everything is built on fundamentals. Fundamentals make up the foundation on which we build our goals. People need to recognize and define their fundamentals, and they should never neglect them. I know that a gymnast without good fundamentals can never make it to the top, and that holds true with almost anything in life. When people feel lost or disjointed, they should just go back to the basics and get back on track. It will lead to peace and longevity.

Always remember that everything is relative. If a double back flip is the hardest skill a gymnast has, then it is going to be the skill that requires the most work, results in the most worry, and probably leads to the most inconsistency. But, if that gymnast starts to work on a triple back flip, improvements there will naturally lead to improvements on the double back. In the process of mastering the triple back flip, the double will seem easy, if not basic, and it will likely be consistent. That goes to show that if possible (and reasonable), people should always try to prepare beyond their necessary level to accomplish their goals. When I was training, I would often try to do longer routines in practice than I was planning to do in competition. Sometimes, I would even add a more difficult skill. That way, when I did my routine in competition, I would feel very confident and secure, knowing I was competing the "easy" routine. Also, if I found myself in a position where I needed to take a risk to get a medal or to achieve my personal goal, I could always attempt that harder routine I had worked on in training. Sure, it might have been risky, it might not have been the routine I had practiced over and over again, but if it gave me a shot at a medal, why not try it? I had practiced it, and I was prepared for anything.

In gymnastics, the goal is to make the hardest skill appear simple. It can be done because presentation is so much a part of the sport, and the best gymnasts master their presentation. In many areas of life, the same principle holds true: presentation is the key! It is not only what someone does, but also how someone does it that counts. People need to learn their crafts well and present them with confidence and authority. Those who are the most confident—the most certain—will hold more power than those with less confidence. In gymnastics, the judges always spotted the competitors with confidence, and it always showed in the scores. So, prepare well, and confidently show the world what you have to offer!

Chapter 18

CONCLUDING THOUGHTS

I believe myself to have been very fortunate in the world of gymnastics. No matter how talented or how strong a gymnast is, there is also an element of luck or good fortune. Even the best athletes in the world have bad days, and if that bad day comes on the day of an important competition, the athlete is out of luck. But in truth, that "luck," or lack thereof, is really a matter of perspective. Each day's success or failure is determined by our outlook, or by what we make of it. Yes, every gymnast dreams of making the Olympic team, and every gymnast dreams of earning those glorious gold medals, of earning the admiration of the spectators and other athletes, and of being known as "the best." But, if that doesn't happen, we must never see ourselves—or our lives—as failures. As long as we have done the best we can do with what we have, we have not failed in the least.

In the movie <u>Cool Runnings</u>, one of the best lines was, "A gold medal is a wonderful thing. But, if you're not enough without it, you'll never be enough with it." Those words are important to keep in mind, no matter what the medal count may be, and no matter what "luck" occurs or doesn't occur on an important day. My years of gymnastics competition brought me lots of success. That is true. I would not want to trade those successes for anything. But, gymnastics has also brought me my principles, my work ethic, the respect I have for others and others have for me, and amazing, life-long friends. Additionally, gymnastics has provided me with my career as an entertainer, it has allowed me to see the world, it has given me empathy and admiration for others, and it has taught me all about cause and effect. Although gymnastics is only a sport, for me, it has been my classroom of life. It has been an invaluable tutor, and it has made me who I am today. I am grateful to God for allowing me to enjoy such an incredible life in the sport, and I am grateful to my family and friends for their understanding and support through all of my experiences in gymnastics.

As I look back now, of course I wonder if I might have been able to do better, or I realize that I could have done worse. But, I have no regrets, for I always did all that I could to make things work out the way I wished for them to. And really, when it comes right down to it, I know that things worked out the way they were meant to. And, for that, to sum it all up, I'm a grateful, happy guy.

Afterthoughts: Personal Mottos and Truths

Anything worth doing is worth doing well. Once you start something, you should always finish it. (My dad told me this, and it has served me all my life. Thanks, Dad.)

If we are lucky, we have eighty to one hundred years of life. Start thinking now about how you want to feel when you look back at your years.

Always try to have something to look forward to.

Recognize progress. Let it feed you.

Work smarter, not harder.

Take time often to evaluate yourself and to appreciate your accomplishments.

When you dread something, it drains you mentally. When you are mentally drained, it drains you physically. Try to enjoy life, not to dread it.

Work for and earn your leisure. If you work hard, believe that it is okay to relax or treat yourself to something nice.

Life should be filled with things we are passionate about. Doing what we are passionate about creates purpose.

Your own will to succeed is more important than anybody else's will for you to succeed.

Success is a by-product of passion and having fun.

Successes should be treasured in the short term. Each success is just a stepping-stone toward the next challenge or opportunity to have more success. The ultimate success is simply to have any success at all.

Model your success from others, and use the success of others to motivate you to create and to surpass.

There is a big difference between taking irresponsible risks and taking calculated risks.

Train harder than you perform.

If you have not failed, you have not lived.

Failures make the best stories.

For every bad attempt I made on a new trick, I was one attempt closer to doing it right.

Pick people's brains. They might share the one phrase, one word, or one idea that is the missing piece to your puzzle.

There are three things we all need: passion, learning, and training.

When we accept a challenge, it brings out the very best that we are.

Don't make excuses. Be honest with yourself. The truth will always find its way to the surface, so don't waste any time trying to keep it buried.

To perfect and to grow in what we do, our efforts must become a habit.

Even thinking a certain way will become a habit over time. We are all self-programmable.

We all have routines. Change your routines if they don't serve you. Create new routines or rituals that will turn into habits that serve you and allow you to serve others.

Evaluate yourself. Determine what makes you tick, what brings you joy, and what makes you proud. Then, pursue those things.

All change takes place in the mind first. Make positive changes by adjusting your thoughts, not by adjusting to the thoughts of others.

The person who is most certain will always influence the person who is less certain.

Somebody always has it worse. Helping others helps yourself.

If you are ever feeling really down, do something for someone else. You will be appreciated, and that appreciation will give you the momentum to get out of your unpleasant rut.

Experience answers questions you don't even know you should ask the first time around. There is no substitute for experience.

Pressure comes from a fear of consequences. Pressure has limits, and the most pressure people can ever feel is the pressure they put on themselves.

Every day counts, so never waste a day. Each day should be used and enjoyed.

Once a day is gone, you can't get it back. Make the most of it. Make it mean something.

Once a moment is gone, you will never have it again. Once an opportunity is gone, it may never return. Keep your eyes open, and appreciate both the good and the bad in life.

Your goal should be to make work something fun—something to look forward to.

Feel grateful. Appreciate life.

57639381R00108

Made in the USA
Lexington, KY
25 November 2016